ANTHONY SCARAMUCCI

SOLANA

RISING

INVESTING
IN THE
FAST LANE
OF *CRYPTO*

WILEY

Published by John Wiley & Sons, Inc., Hoboken, New Jersey.
Published simultaneously in Canada.

For general information on our other products and services or for technical support, please contact our Customer Care Department within the United States at (800) 762-2974, outside the United States at (317) 572-3993 or fax (317) 572-4002.

Wiley also publishes its books in a variety of electronic formats. Some content that appears in print may not be available in electronic formats. For more information about Wiley products, visit our web site at www.wiley.com.

Library of Congress Cataloging-in-Publication Data is Available:

ISBN 9781394358595 (Cloth)
ISBN 9781394358601 (ePub)
ISBN 9781394358618 (ePDF)

COVER DESIGN: PAUL MCCARTHY
Printed and bound by CPI Group (UK) Ltd, Croydon, CR0 4YY

C9781394358595_111025

Contents

Foreword

by Kyle Samani, Founder of Multicoin Capital

I was the first and largest investor in Solana, and I have been working closely with founders Anatoly Yakovenko and Raj Gokal since the earliest days. We lived through the highest of highs, like Summer of Solana, and the lowest of lows, including the collapse of FTX, something we now look back on as trauma bonding.

I have had the opportunity to speak with almost every L1 and L2 founder in crypto in the last ~10 years, so when I first met Anatoly and Raj, I knew they were different.

First, Anatoly was not an academic; instead, he drew on his experiences building high-performance systems at companies like Qualcomm and Dropbox. Virtually all the other L1 founders of the 2018 era proudly showcased their academic credentials. Anatoly was the opposite. I found that refreshing.

Second, Anatoly made it clear that he did not want to innovate technically. Earlier in his career, he had tried to solve unsolved computer science problems and failed. He promised himself he'd never do that again and, after a period of time, vowed to focus only on using established techniques to boost system performance and outcome.

Third, Anatoly had a clear vision from the start. He wanted Solana to power a decentralized version of the Nasdaq, the stock market that revolutionized trading with electronic systems. His goal was a global platform for capital markets, open to everyone, everywhere, with instant, real-time data. This would free investors from the restrictive, centralized, traditional finance exchanges of the past.

This approach was bold and unique; none of Anatoly's peers had such a clear focus. While others aimed to scale blockchains without pinpointing specific goals, Anatoly zeroed in on a concrete problem. Frustrated by the slow, laggy data from Interactive Brokers, he set out to build Solana as a system that delivers instant, permissionless access to real-time market data for anyone, anywhere in the world.

Fourth, Anatoly and Raj prioritized enabling developers on Solana to generate revenue. This seems straightforward, but in 2018, when crypto was fixated on pure decentralization, their practical focus was unique. I found their commitment to creating tangible earning opportunities for developers both refreshing and visionary.

Ultimately, Solana's success hinged on these distinct qualities. It was a classic startup: scrappy, innovative, and lean. Anatoly and Raj worked to define the minimum viable product—the simplest version of Solana that could deliver real value—and focused on finding product-market fit, meaning uses that people actually needed. While many crypto projects lost sight of the focus required for startups to thrive, Anatoly and Raj embedded these principles into Solana's core from the very beginning.

I've been working with Anatoly and Raj for more than seven years. They have become fabulously wealthy, but they still continue to fight every day. They still get their hands dirty, working with developers, testing applications, and cultivating the Solana ecosystem. And they've hired and built a stellar global organization, too.

The rest of this book will provide a detailed history of Solana and the people and companies that made its success possible. But before you read on, I'd like to share my thoughts for the future of crypto, and Solana's role in it.

Crypto systems have many unique properties, but the most important is that they enable people to self-custody financial assets. As eloquently articulated by Yuval Noah Harari in Sapiens, financial assets do not exist in the realm of physics; they exist only in the realm of human fiction. Up until the advent of crypto, the fiction was rooted in government trust (either in the form of fiat or in the form of securities laws). Crypto enables humanity to have a global shared fiction that is rooted not in a government but in physics.

Crypto, at its core, is about freedom. It's about owning your money in a way that's never been possible before. Forget banks or governments holding your assets hostage. Solana lets you self-custody your wealth, take it anywhere, and do whatever you want with it. Gift it, trade it, and use it as collateral, anytime, anywhere with no middleman or borders.

Solana's built to move value at lightning-fast speed, whether you're buying coffee or trading billions in assets. It's collapsing commerce and Wall Street into one global, permissionless system. This has profound implications for global capital flows, access to financial markets, and commerce around the world. Crypto is strictly necessary for capitalism to permeate every last corner of the planet.

On the surface, crypto might seem like a casino, but don't be fooled by the wild prices swing, Meme activity, and at times chaotic vibe. Crypto, and Solana in particular, is shaking up the core rules of how money and society work. Crypto tackles hidden flaws in the traditional financial system that most people, especially in the United States, rarely notice. Yet those flaws hit hard in critical moments, especially when it's your money on the line.

Solana's mission is to power global Internet capital markets, making financial opportunities accessible to everyone, everywhere. When money can move instantly and freely across the Internet, it creates a new kind of market, one that's already taking shape. Today, billions of dollars flow through Solana's blockchain daily, and with new laws like the GENIUS and CLARITY acts, I'm confident we'll see that soar to trillions per day in the coming years.

Money is nothing, and simultaneously everything. Soon everyone in the world will have access to global money on Solana.

Preface

When I was kid, I used to watch *Star Trek* and call BS on Photon Phaser. No way! Would never happen. Teleportation? Yeah right. Flying cars? Still waiting. The future depicted in 1960s science fiction felt like a distant mirage, a realm of fantastical technologies. In *2001: A Space Odyssey*, I saw talking telephones and HAL 9000, a computer with a voice and a mind of its own. These visions of tomorrow seemed impossibly far off, but a curious thing happened on the way to the future. Many of those things came true. FaceTime, which would've been unthinkable just decades ago, is now part of our daily lives. In fact, much of what was considered fantasy is now fact. We are living in the future of our past, standing on the cusp of a reality that would rival those depicted in cinematic fantasies. The Photon isn't here, for now at least, but other technologies are changing the world in which we live and work. And one of the most transformative technologies changing the face of money and commerce is the blockchain.

Blockchain technology is the foundation of a new economic paradigm. Period. Full stop. Bitcoin, the pioneer, was a quantum leap forward. It introduced the idea of a decentralized payment network that digitized value and created the equivalent of digital gold. For the first time, anyone, anywhere, could transfer value across the globe in a frictionless, instantaneous fashion, free of intermediaries. This was a paradigm shift for money itself, endowing individuals with financial sovereignty. No government. No banks. Just put pure blockchain. Following Bitcoin's trailblazing path, Ethereum took the revolution further. It introduced programmable money through smart contracts, enabling anyone to build businesses atop a decentralized, open-source network. Ethereum transformed the blockchain into a platform for creating economies, fostering innovation, and empowering entrepreneurs worldwide. It was a second seismic shift, proving that blockchain technology could extend beyond simple payments and stores of value to redefine how we structure and scale commerce. Simply put, if Bitcoin represents the early Internet, functional but limited, then Ethereum represents the companies built on top of it, the Amazons and Netflixes of the world.

Now, a new chapter is unfolding with Solana, a blockchain so revolutionary it is unlocking possibilities once deemed unimaginable. Solana is the iPhone of blockchains. It's scalable, fast, and cheap, and its technology is redefining what a blockchain can achieve. Solana is a foundation for building companies that are reshaping commerce. Solana enables the creation of entirely new businesses and networks, transforming how we trade, invest, and interact with assets. From art to real estate to intellectual property and to financial instruments, Solana is digitizing and liquefying assets of all kinds, making them accessible, tradable, and dynamic in ways previously thought impossible. Solana is driving a new economy, one where decentralized networks empower individuals and businesses to innovate without the constraints of traditional systems.

Its blockchain is the promise of tomorrow. It is the real example of science-fiction fantasies. And to me, it represented a generational investment opportunity.

I wrote this book, my second on crypto, to tell the story of the visionaries who built Solana and continue to push its boundaries. These are the stories of the people who saw the potential of the blockchain to change lives, democratize wealth, and create systems that are fairer, more transparent, and more accessible. They are builders of a virtual future on which the economies of tomorrow will rest. They are building global opportunities.

Bitcoin was a once-in-a-generation trade, the investment equivalent of Halley's Comet. It transformed my firm, positioning us as forward-thinking asset managers and ambassadors to a new financial world. When I first bought Bitcoin, I believed it was a singular moment, a generational investment that would go on to define my career. After all, how could one reasonably expect to repeat such a great trade? Then came Solana. It has offered me and my firm a second chance at a once-in-a-lifetime opportunity. Solana combines the best of both Bitcoin and Ethereum, and our involvement has cemented SkyBridge's place at the forefront of innovation, ensuring we remain leaders in a rapidly evolving landscape.

This book is an invitation to you, the reader, to understand and seize this moment, too. After reading it, you will understand how Solana is reshaping how we live, work, and interact. The stories within these pages illuminate the path forward, showing how Solana is enabling entrepreneurs, creators, and investors to build a future that is decentralized, inclusive, and dynamic. You will learn how to own it, use it, and build on it. You will understand why it was able to overcome numerous near-death experiences and why its journey is just beginning. You will learn the story of its founders and its early investors and the numerous challenges they overcame to create this incredible network. Most of all, you'll have a front row seat to a classic David versus Goliath tale.

We may not have flying cars, and teleportation seems a bit off, but the blockchain has brought to focus a future far more advanced than we ever could have imagined. The possibilities are endless. The technology is limitless. I was fortunate to ride the Bitcoin wave, and now, with Solana, I see a second chance to shape the future. After reading this book, I hope you, too, will recognize the opportunity. And seize it.

Chapter 1

The Crypto Meteor

Sam Bankman-Fried (SBF) leaned forward, his voice cutting through the hum of the penthouse dining room.

"What went down that day when the mobile brokers, Robinhood, the whole lot, yanked the plug on retail trading for those tickers?"

The dinner table went quiet, the kind of quiet that makes you notice the small sounds. SBF's knee was going to town under the table, a constant thump-thump-thump that sounded like an animal trying to free itself from a cage. His eyes, half-hidden behind a mop of hair that looked like it had never met a comb, darted around the room, up, down, sideways, never quite landing on anyone for more than a split second. You could feel the skyline glittering through the windows of the 56th floor at Hudson Yards, but SBF's twitchy gaze was the real spectacle.

"Like, why did they freeze it?"

He didn't wait for an answer. In the same breath, he launched into the GameStop saga, when an army of retail traders, armed with Reddit threads and margin accounts, took on the Wall Street machine. It wasn't just a story; it was a new line drawn in the foundation of finance, a glimpse of a world where the little guy could take on and beat the establishment at its game, and SBF was narrating the opening salvo.

It was September 2021, and the occasion was the dinner following the SkyBridge SALT Conference, my firm's annual gathering that, in years past, had been held at the Bellagio in Las Vegas. SALT was a magnet for the cultural elite, the kind of event where you might spot a hedge fund titan swapping stories with a celebrity or a sitting senator. COVID had sidelined it in 2020, but now it was back and relocated to the heart of Manhattan, the nation's ground zero for COVID. The city was clawing its way out of the pandemic, and SALT's return felt like a victory lap. This dinner, held in a $50 million penthouse, was the culmination of that comeback, taking place in a room full of investors, visionaries, and one frenetic 29-year-old crypto wunderkind who seemed to vibrate at his own frequency.

The question hung in the air, unanswered.

"Why *did* they freeze it?"

SBF's knee kept pounding, and the silence stretched, but you could tell he already knew the answer, or at least thought he did. In his world, the old rules were crumbling, and he was ready to build something new on the rubble.

Tonight's dinner was different from previous ones. It was a collision of worlds, a moment when the old titans of Wall Street rubbed shoulders with the next generation of financial leaders. The past was crashing into the future. SkyBridge, the firm I'd built from the ground up in 2005, had always been a place for big ideas, but this? This was bold. It was our debut conference as a Bitcoin and crypto player, a pivot we'd announced earlier in 2020, and we were hosting the first major financial conference in New York since the pandemic had turned the world upside down. The stakes felt higher, the room felt stranger, and the possibilities felt bigger.

The usual suspects were there, hedge fund royalty and asset allocators who'd spent decades inventing and mastering new markets.

But this time, they weren't the only ones commanding attention. The crypto crowd had arrived, and they didn't look or talk like anyone else in the room. Steve Cohen, the hedge fund legend whose S.A.C. Capital had rewritten the rules of the game, sat there, motionless, with a bemused smile on his face, his usual swagger replaced by something closer to awe. Dan Loeb, the sharp-tongued maestro of Third Point, who could pen a lacerating letter to a CEO in the morning and then quote Kafka over vegan sushi by lunch, was uncharacteristically quiet, his jaw practically on the floor as he watched a kid in baggy shorts and a wrinkled T-shirt, knees bouncing like he'd had one too many Red Bulls, explain a trillion-dollar idea with the casual confidence of a professional magician.

But unlike years past, these Wall Street titans were joined by a new crop of investors eager to snatch the unofficial crown of Wall Street's new Masters of the Universe. Pantera's Dan Morehead, a grizzled Wall Street trader turned crypto king, held court in one corner. And then there were Anatoly Yakovenko and Raj Gokal, the brains behind Solana Labs, who'd later tip me off to the second-best investment I'd ever make. The new breed wasn't the polished pitchmen of traditional finance, but they surely did have a story to tell. The old guard were traders with catlike reflexes and a gift for spotting and quickly devouring fleeting glimpses of value. The new guys were builders, dreamers, and people who spoke in code and saw the world not as it was but for what it could be.

And then there was SBF, the disheveled prodigy of the moment. "Look, you'll find all sorts of GameStop conspiracy theories online," he said, softly looking up at the ceiling as if to signal the ridiculousness of it all. "None of 'em make sense. What happened shows why crypto works." The room leaned in, eager to be let in on the secret, not so much about the Meme stock crash day, about which they knew plenty, but about something much, much bigger. It was the future, messy and raw, taking shape right before their eyes.

SBF had the most unusual and jarring way of communicating, a kind of tangle of cascading contradictions. He could unravel the most arcane financial concepts with the clarity of an MIT professor, but the words tumbled out in a chaotic stream of Valley Girl–like "ums," "likes," and nervous giggles punctuated by a jittery knee that seemed to have its own agenda. The effect was disorienting, like watching a master chef whip up a gourmet dish using nothing but a jar of Heinz ketchup and Ritz crackers. And yet, somehow, it worked, brilliantly.

For the next hour, SBF, as the world knew him, held the room in a trance. The press had slapped a bunch of grandiose and lazy labels on him. "Warren Buffett of Bitcoin," "J.P. Morgan of Crypto," but I never paid much attention to those monikers. The easy analogies sold his brilliance short. Still, when he spoke, you listened, because he wasn't just explaining crypto; he was revealing the future. And his future did not include the creaky, clunky machinery of stock trading, a system most people assumed was as solid as rock.

"Think about it," he said, his tone half-lecture, half-stand-up routine. "You go on your phone, buy a share of Amazon, and you're like, 'Cool, I own it'. Except it takes *two friggin'* days to actually get it. And in those two days, that share passes through, what, 10 different companies? *Ten!*" He paused, letting the number hang in the air like some sort of insult. "You don't think about that when you're on Robinhood or E★TRADE, right? You see the little stock icon on your screen, and you're like, 'Yup, that's mine'. But those companies? They're just a forward-facing brokers. They're not the exchange, not the clearinghouse, not the market maker."

The room was dead silent, forks frozen mid-bite, iPhones untouched. SBF's knee kept bouncing, a constant drum of nervous energy. "So, for like 48 hours, you think you own that share. Your account says you do. But really, you're just hoping those 10 companies don't screw it up. You're trusting that none of them goes, 'Whoops, sorry, we lost your share, good luck!'" He flashed a sheepish grin. "That's the dirty secret of the stock market. It's like that trust fall game you play at camp," referencing the game where you back backward into the arms of a campmate, "but just with a dozen strangers."

He barreled on, his cadence picking up steam, his eyes now darting like they were chasing his own thoughts. "Now, let's say that share of Amazon jumps a hundred bucks the first day. You're up 100, right? Except you're not, because the trade is not settled yet. If one of those 10 players fumbles, poof! Your profit is gone. And every one of those companies knows this, so they've got to keep a giant pile of cash, what they call 'regulatory capital', just in case someone drops the ball. It's like everyone's hedging against everyone else's incompetence."

By now, his knee was practically a blur, as if it were acting out the frantic handoffs of a stock settlement, broker to clearinghouse to transfer agent, each step a potential fumble. The audience was riveted, not because SBF was polished (he was not) but because he'd taken something as mundane as buying a stock and turned it into a high-stakes game of financial Russian roulette. In his telling, the stock market wasn't a bedrock of capitalism. It was like some rickety Jenga tower, one bad pull from collapse. And crypto? That was the fix, the sleek new system that could do in seconds what Wall Street took days to fumble through. He didn't need to say it outright. The room got the message. The future was here, and it was wearing cargo shorts. The Wall Street titans, the ones who could dissect a balance sheet in their sleep, sat there, in a state of quiet wonder, like they'd just been told a carnival barker rigged the market. It was like finding out your bulletproof vest was made of Kleenex.

SBF was just getting started, and now he was really going to rock their world. "On that day," he continued, his voice a bit more focused, "those retail kids made so much money, they burned through the capital reserves of the weakest links in the clearing chain. Poof! Firms froze. Trades halted. Liquidations started. Why? Because if those traders kept winning, the system might not deliver.

Your profits? Gone. Your account? Zeroed out. That's not a market. That's a shit show."

He paused, letting the room stew in its own discomfort. These were the masters of the universe, guys who'd shorted the housing market, dodged the '08 crash, and still had their Hamptons estates. And here was this kid, in baggy shorts, telling them their world was a house of cards.

"But you know what didn't break that day?" SBF said, his voice rising, eyes glinting like he was going to let them in on a little secret. "While the stock market was choking on GameStop, while clearinghouses were hitting the panic button, you know what kept trading, no hiccups, no freezes, just pure, chaotic volume?" He stretched the word out, "Dogggeeee-coin," like he was savoring the absurdity.

The room laughed, nervous and disbelieving. Dogecoin? The crypto joke with a Shiba Inu mascot, dreamed up by two coders in 2013 to mock the Bitcoin hype? The coin Elon Musk had turned into a cultural relic by tweeting about it in the middle of the night? That Dogecoin? "Yeah," SBF said, grinning. "That thing settled just fine. Instant trades, no middleman, no meltdown. Blockchain."

The point landed like a gut punch. Wall Street's plumbing—its clearinghouses, its settlement systems—was creaking under pressure. Meanwhile, a cartoon dog coin, built on tech most of these guys had never heard of, was humming along. SBF's message was clear; the old world of equities was a dinosaur, and crypto, with its blockchains, was the meteor. Instant settlement. No counterparty risk. A system that didn't need a suit in a corner office to function.

Now, SBF was no saint. A year later, his empire, FTX, would implode in a spectacular mess of hubris, bad accounting, and missing billions. I'd later learn that the hard way, with my own firm caught in the fallout and my reputation collateral damage. But that night, in front of a room full of Wall Street's elite, SBF was a prophet.

He saw the matrix of crypto—its tech, its promise, its flaws—clearer than anyone. And he wasn't just selling a dream; he was explaining a revolution.

Fortunately, it was a revolution my firm and I joined a year earlier. In December 2020, I made the call to pivot SkyBridge, my fund of funds shop, from Wall Street asset manager to crypto firm. We'd been pioneers, pooling smaller sums of money to give investors access to the best and brightest hedge funds in the world, Ray Dalio's Bridgewater and David Tepper's Appaloosa. But by 2020, that game was crowded. Copycats were everywhere. The edge was gone. Crypto, though? That was the new frontier. Bitcoin wasn't just digital gold; it was digital value. Portable, incorruptible, immune to the Fed's money-printing binge. Blockchain wasn't a buzzword; it was a paradigm shift.

The Street wasn't ready. Warren Buffett called Bitcoin "rat poison squared." Jamie Dimon sneered it was a "pet rock." They weren't wrong about the risks. Those early days were rife with hacks, scams, and crashes that could make a grown trader cry. But the naysayers missed the bigger picture. Since 2008, central banks had been flooding the world with cash, devaluing every dollar in your wallet. The Fed wasn't just a policy wonk's problem anymore; it was a Main Street issue. People felt the squeeze, with groceries pricier and wages flat. Occupy Wall Street, the Tea Party, the rage at "the system"? That was the spark. Bitcoin was the resulting fire.

When COVID hit and the Fed pulled out the same crisis playbook, money printers went into overdrive, and the case for crypto went from compelling to screaming. My firm's bet on Bitcoin didn't just pay off; it obliterated the market. We weren't just ahead of the curve; we were drawing a new one. SkyBridge became a literal bridge to this wild, lucrative world, guiding traditional investors through the crypto jungle. We were more than just investors; we were ambassadors. And at the conclusion of every SALT, we hosted a small dinner with our top clients, only now, many of those were from the world of the coin.

That night, as SBF held court, one skeptic piped up. "Okay, Sam, outside of Bitcoin. But what's the next big thing in crypto?"

SBF didn't blink. "Solana," he said. "The winner will be the fastest, cheapest system you can trust. That's the winner. That's Solana."

Solana. The name hit like a sunbeam. If Bitcoin was Apple in 2007, Solana was Nvidia in 2012—raw, unpolished, brimming with potential. Solana wasn't just a coin; it was a network, a platform for apps, NFTs, DeFi, all moving at light speed. For SkyBridge, it was our next moonshot.

The story of Solana, and the brilliant people who built it, is the story of a generational trade. It's not just about tech or money; it's about rewriting the rules of finance. In the pages ahead, you'll meet the visionaries, the coders, and the colorful characters who made it all happen. You'll see why Solana is not just a bet; it's a glimpse of the future. And you'll learn how to use and invest in ways you never thought possible.

Hang tight. I'm going to take you on the ride of your life.

Chapter 2

Ethereum Killers

Kyle Samani was practically brimming with excitement, and it wasn't the margaritas or the balmy Cancun breeze. It was November 2017, the air still thick with the festive remnants of Día de los Muertos, Mexico's version of Halloween. Skeletons and marigold streamers littered the Cancun International Convention Center like the aftermath of a particularly macabre prom. Samani, a 20-something ex-Google coder with a mop of dark hair and smooth olive skin, was one of 2,000 crypto zealots packed into the Ethereum developer's conference. The place buzzed with the kind of fervor you'd expect from people who believed they were on the cusp of the next great investment, one that would make them rich beyond their dreams and maybe even change civilization itself.

Samani was a newcomer to the money management game, having just launched Multicoin Capital, his crypto hedge fund, months earlier. He wasn't your typical Wall Street guy; he was a tech guy who'd stumbled into what he thought was the future. Ethereum, to him, wasn't just a cryptocurrency. It was the Internet's second act, a programmable blockchain that made

Bitcoin look like a pocket calculator. Bitcoin was a ledger for moving digital cash, clever but limited. Ethereum? It was a global supercomputer, a decentralized beast that could run smart contracts, self-executing code that could power anything from virtual stock markets to ride-sharing apps without a corporate middleman. Samani saw it as the scaffolding for a new world, one where you could rebuild Uber or Airbnb on a network that no one owned. "Why do you need a company?" he'd ask investors and friends. "The blockchain connects the drivers and riders. Done."

But Ethereum had a problem, and it wasn't a small one. For all its sci-fi promise, it was slow, glacial even. Its proof-of-work system, a clunky relic of Bitcoin's design, capped the network to 15–30 transactions per second. Visa, by comparison, could handle thousands. Every 12 seconds, Ethereum's network churned out a new block of transactions, but those blocks were tiny, capped to keep the system decentralized. When too many people tried to use it, the network clogged like a rush-hour freeway. Users had to pay "gas fees," a processing fee that acted like a tax just to get their transactions through, and during peak times, those fees could spike to absurd levels, $50, $100, or more just to move some digital tokens. It was like paying a toll booth in gold bars. Samani knew Ethereum needed to get faster and cheaper without losing the security and decentralization that made it special. That's why he was in Cancun, crammed into a convention hall with coders, dreamers, and a few sharp-eyed journalists. He wanted to hear how Ethereum was going to improve and grow. He wanted to get a glimpse of its future.

The star of the show was Vitalik Buterin, Ethereum's 23-year-old co-founder, a gangly Russian-Canadian with short-cut hair and a brain that seemed wired to a different dimension. In crypto circles, Buterin was a demigod, a wunderkind who'd supposedly taught himself Mandarin in months and lived like a monk despite a net worth in the billions. Stories about him bordered on myth.

He ate whole lemons, peel and all. He carried his life in a suitcase. He looked like he'd been designed by a 3D printer set to robot mode. His origin story was pure crypto lore. Introduced to Bitcoin at 17 by his software engineer dad, Vitalik initially scoffed at the industry, dismissing it as a fad. He was more into video games and the World of Warcraft than digital money. But something clicked, maybe his distrust of governments, hardened from growing up in post-Soviet Russia, or maybe just the sheer math of it all. By 2011, he was writing for Bitcoin blogs, earning pocket change in coins worth less than $100 each. Buterin juggled this with classes at the University of Waterloo. He was a loner whose freakish intellect had always set him apart. Schoolyard cliques never got him. He instead found solace in the digital deep end, far from the noise of pop culture. He co-founded Bitcoin Magazine and dropped out of college, and by 2013, he was crisscrossing the globe.

To Buterin's mind, Bitcoin's blockchain was a one-trick pony, good for only tracking digital cash. He wanted more. He wanted a platform where developers could build anything, from financial markets to social networks, all running on a decentralized digital infrastructure. In May 2013, Silicon Valley hosted the first big US Bitcoin summit, organized by the Bitcoin Foundation to sell businesses and dreamers on the coin's potential. Cameron and Tyler Winklevoss, the handsome twins immortalized as the Winklevii in *The Social Network*, headlined the event. The film chronicled their Harvard feud with Mark Zuckerberg, who they claimed stole their idea for an online Facebook. They settled for a cool $220 million, and by 2013, with Bitcoin hovering around $250 a coin, they sunk enough into it to claim an $11 million stake, worth more than $3 billion today. The movie made them crypto's rock stars, and they leaned in, preaching Bitcoin's gospel. The summit buzzed with gizmos, Bitcoin ATMs, wallets, payment platforms, some so clunky they seemed doomed to fail. But the crowd's fervor was electric, and for Buterin, it was a revelation. After that, he never went back to school.

That summer, Buterin became a crypto nomad, bouncing from London to Israel to San Francisco, grilling anyone tinkering with Bitcoin's blockchain. Most were slapping new, what engineers called "layers" on it, chasing speed and versatility (more on this later). To Buterin, that approach was like bolting a V8 engine onto a 1960s Mercedes tourer. It was a clunky retrofit, the blockchain version of MTV's *Pimp My Ride*. Bitcoin, built by the mysterious Satoshi Nakamoto was a vault, not a sports car. Safe, secure, not flashy.

Buterin had a wilder idea: a new network, a Bitcoin 2.0, with Turing-complete programming (named for Alan Turing, the genius engineer whose work birthed modern computing a century before). This blockchain wouldn't just move money; it could host entire markets, social platforms, and digital commerce, all free from government meddling. A frictionless world of code, data, and audacity. He poured his vision into a whitepaper, naming it Ethereum, a nod to the sci-fi ether once thought to carry light through the cosmos, with an "-eum" suffix for poetic flair. It sounded clean, vast, like the universe itself, decentralized and infinite. He fired it off to a few friends, who pinged it to dozens more. The buzz was instant.

In January 2014, Buterin pitched Ethereum at the North American Bitcoin Conference in Miami. The crowd, obsessed with Bitcoin's next act, barely noticed the scrawny kid with no tech giant on his résumé. A new blockchain? Ambitious, particularly for a 19-year-old betting on a future most doubted existed; it was downright nuts. Some scoffed. Others saw genius.

But Buterin kept talking. His "smart contract" platform could stretch blockchain beyond payments or digital gold. It could power a new economy, a Web 3.0. Think AOL in the 90s, clunky but connective, spawning Web 2.0 giants like Instagram and Netflix, unimaginable until they weren't. Ethereum could be that next leap. Skeptics scoffed, but the idea of programmable money sparked something. The crowd started to listen. The idea took root, and by 2015, Ethereum was live, a scrappy underdog to Bitcoin's heavyweight title.

That's what drew Samani to Cancun in 2017—the promise of the next great idea that would grow this wondrous new network. Perhaps because of that promise and the direct result of its rising popularity, Ethereum enthusiasts faced several frustrating challenges in 2017. Rapid adoption laid bare some of the platform's technical limitations. Ethereum's blockchain was brilliant, but it struggled to handle the growing number of transactions on the network. It was as if someone had created an excellent streaming service, and as its popularity fueled a surge in traffic, the network simply couldn't keep up. Slower transactions meant higher gas fees, which in turn only heightened developers' sense of frustration. Those higher gas fees created a barrier for developers of lesser means. Interacting with Ethereum's network could also prove clunky for all but the best engineers. Finally, there was a lingering sense that the network was slow to upgrade. Everyone was aware of the network's problems, but few seemed willing to offer any clarity about how to address them and move forward. How were they going to address issues of scalability? Efficiency?

Still, the network continued to grow despite its self-inflicted problems. Competing blockchains popped up, but they'd go away just as quickly, a fleeting flash in the crypto pan. Still, the true believers who swore their allegiance to Ethereum, flawed as it was, stuck with it. Ethereum in 2017 was like Yahoo in 2006, dominant and brilliant but deeply flawed, poorly run, and seemingly unable to change and harness its true power. But the faithful held out hope. And Samani was one of them.

Now, a couple years later in Cancun, Samani sat in the front row, his heart pounding like he was about to see a rock star. The conference was electric, the biggest yet. Buterin was set to speak, and Samani was desperate for a signal that Ethereum could fix its flaws, namely, scalability, speed, and those stubbornly high gas fees. The stage was a parade of engineers and crypto investors, but when Buterin finally shuffled up, the room went still. He looked like he'd just rolled out of a hostel bunk, hair disheveled, his voice a rapid-fire monotone that barely paused for breath. He rattled off Ethereum's growth: from a $70 million market cap to $28 billion. He tossed out buzzwords like "sharding," a technique that splits the blockchain into smaller, faster pieces (more on that later) and "proof of stake," a greener alternative to the energy-hogging "proof of work" that Bitcoin relied on. He called it a "modest proposal," but there was no wit, no life, no excitement, just a dense thicket of jargon. "Let's keep pushing forward together!" he said, curtly waving and just as quickly vanishing offstage.

Samani blinked.

That was it? He'd come for a roadmap, a battle plan to make Ethereum the backbone of a new economy. Instead, he got a history lesson and vague promises. No timelines, no specifics, just the same cautious optimism he'd heard for years. It felt like Ethereum, the rebel upstart, had turned into a lumbering corporation, paralyzed by its own success. Samani's stomach churned. Multicoin, his fledgling fund, was all in on Ethereum, a bet that now felt like a losing one. He'd poured everything into this vision, a world where blockchains replaced boardrooms, where code was king. He left the convention center dejected and depressed, in stark contrast to the festive skulls and streamers that seemed to mock his mood. He couldn't shake the feeling that he'd bet on a dream that was about to turn into his worst nightmare.

What drove him really nuts was the lost potential. The idea for Ethereum was so singularly brilliant that you couldn't help but want to invest in it. Bitcoin, by contrast, never appealed to Samani. Dumb by design, its only defining feature was its 21 million coins, he'd tell colleagues. Bitcoin never changed. That's why people liked it. In Samani's view, Bitcoin was just a store of value. Digital gold would appeal to a specific group of investors, but its real power was that it never changed at all. It wasn't programmable.

It didn't scale. It was slow and expensive to use. He didn't believe in owning what he called non-productive assets and would channel Warren Buffett (ironically, Crypto Public Enemy #1) and his hatred for gold.

"Gold gets dug out of the ground in Africa or someplace. Then we melt it down, dig another hole, bury it again, and pay people to guard it. It has no utility. Anyone watching from Mars would be scratching their head," Buffett famously once said, and Samani wholeheartedly agreed. He preferred to buy businesses that produced cash flow. Think Apple and Microsoft. He hated buying something that depended on others to bid it higher. He liked businesses that had the potential to grow, scale, and throw off cash.

I understand Samani's sentiment, but I might take issue with this point. Bitcoin has been one of the greatest investments of all time, and its blockchain technology laid the foundation for all that followed. However, I also understand and appreciate that the universe of crypto investors is large enough to accommodate contrasting views on various protocols. Some people prefer value to growth stocks. Others prefer stocks to bonds. No one is right, and every investor has different skill sets and needs. Some understand certain asset classes better than others. In this regard, few people understand programmable protocols better than Samani. That he didn't like Bitcoin didn't make him right or wrong. It just wasn't his thing.

And at that moment in time, it was becoming clear that Buterin may not be Samani's thing either.

After leaving the conference, Samani decided that Buterin and the people around him were either clueless or arrogant, or perhaps both. They thought they had this monopoly, this moat around their business. They didn't, as far as Samani was concerned. It was only a matter of time before someone would come in and leave Ethereum in the dust. He'd seen this picture before as a former Google engineer and finance student. BlackBerry displaced Palm. Apple destroyed BlackBerry. TV displaced radio, which in turn was destroyed by the Internet. History doesn't repeat. It rhymes. If these Ethereum guys didn't feel any urgency to disrupt themselves, maybe it was time to find some group that did.

So, he set out to find an alternative. At the time, there was no shortage of programmable layer 1 blockchains hitting the market, although most of all it had many flaws. But Samani kept looking. By his thinking, displacing Ethereum was a layup. Surely, some hungry programmers out there felt the same as he did. Of course, there were thousands of engineers, but each project he examined, and even some he invested in, lacked the intellectual or monetary capital to compete. Even projects that had raised millions, and there were quite a few, still struggled to compete against the more established blockchains. For all its flaws, Ethereum was still the leading innovative smart-contract platform. Case closed. It was Pepsi, a clear number two to Coke, but firmly established in second place.

One platform that did catch his attention was EOS, which Block.one launched in 2018. It tried to address many of Ethereum's shortfalls, particularly speed and cost. As a layer 1 blockchain, EOS was probably the most legitimate competitor to Ethereum, and investor enthusiasm was intense. Its initial coin offering in 2017 raised more than $4 billion, but it fizzled over time. Of course, there were others such as Cardano, Tezos, and Tron. While each had defining and innovative features, none posed a serious challenge to Ethereum's dominance, much to Samani's chagrin. Same story. Same result.

But that all changed when he reconnected with Vinny Lingham.

Lingham, a South African-born serial entrepreneur with an infectious smile and forward-thinking spirit, was looking for the same thing as Samani: an Ethereum killer. And he thought he may have found the answer. Lingham had extensive experience in crypto and blockchains, having co-founded Civic, a blockchain identity startup, and was an early and vociferous advocate for Bitcoin and various blockchains. In fact, his early and often correct price predictions earned him the moniker "The Bitcoin Oracle." Residents of South Africa might recognize him as one of the "sharks" on that country's syndicated version of *Shark Tank*. He was an early investor in Multicoin and joined the firm as a general partner in 2017. Samani and Lingham met through their shared interest in crypto, having attended many of the same conferences and events. Lingham was about to introduce Samani to the person who would change his life: Anatoly Yakovenko.

Chapter 3

Decentralized Nasdaq

"I'm going to build a decentralized Nasdaq," said Anatoly Yakovenko before flashing a mischievous grin. It was April 2018, and Kyle Samani's professional life was about to take a massive turn.

After Lingham arranged several introductory phone calls, Samani agreed to meet with Yakovenko at a nondescript shared office space in San Francisco. Lingham loved technical founders. He felt they lived and breathed their companies more than hired guns. Their creation was like their baby. They would spend night and day thinking about it and knew every conceivable wrinkle. And in Yakovenko, Lingham thought he might have found someone who was smart and crazy enough to challenge Ethereum. It took Samani all of five minutes to know he had found the right guy.

"I'm going to build a decentralized Nasdaq. I want to have an on-chain order book. I want to put limit orders on the blockchain," said Yakovenko.

Despite spending the first decade of his life in Ukraine, Yakovenko spoke perfect, nearly unaccented English. With his trimmed beard and short-cut hair, he looked more the part of a surfer, which he loved to do, than a genius computer programmer. But his grasp of technology and finance was more significant than anyone Samani had ever met. He was brilliant. He was motivated. He was the guy.

Yakovenko proposed a system that mirrored traditional markets like the Nasdaq or New York Stock Exchange, but for a virtual, "decentralized" world. In this world, financial assets would operate without a central controlling authority to manage or clear trades. Instead, this system would run on a blockchain. No single party would have ultimate control. A distributed network of nodes would validate and confirm each transaction on an "on-chain" order book. In a traditional exchange, a market maker's order book lists all the bids and offers. When investors want to buy a stock or security, they simply look at the price that is being offered by the market maker, referred to as the "offer." When they want to sell, they look at the market's bid, or what market makers are willing to pay to buy something. The difference between the two is the "bid-ask spread."

In Yakovenko's world, this order book would reside on the blockchain, and the responsibility for ensuring it was updated would fall to the network participants, not the market makers, as is done in every traditional financial (TradFi, as the kids call it) exchange. What he proposed was revolutionary and touched on the promise of decentralized blockchains. Bitcoin virtualized gold, creating digital property. Now, Yakovenko wanted to take it to the next level. He wanted to virtualize trading and turn a centralized activity into a decentralized one. He wanted to create a system that might one day replace the institutions that have been the world's gatekeepers of capital for the last century.

Disruption on Wall Street is not a new concept. After all, electronic trading moved commerce off the stodgy floors of the New York Stock Exchange and the Chicago Mercantile decades ago. Before that, trading was a physical affair, where actual size and physical stature could make the difference between a placed or lost order. Traders would jockey like Sumo wrestlers, pushing, shoving, and screaming in an effort to gain a quarter of a point, five days a week from 9:30 a.m. to 4 p.m. With activity so intense, it was little wonder trading had to stop. They would die if they didn't. The growth of electronic trading gave birth to after-hours trading, and as it became easier to trade, trading hours began to stretch far before and after the bell. Now, there's even 24-hour trading in many stocks.

What Yakovenko was proposing was radical, but it wasn't crazy. It just leveraged and extended the existing power of the blockchain. On-chain trading proposes executing trades directly on the blockchain using an on-chain order book. It would eliminate intermediaries, of which there are still too many, and reduce costs. It would increase speed and accuracy and democratize centralized trading. In Yakovenko's visionary world of virtual trading, anyone, anywhere, could trade assets as seamlessly as they would on the Nasdaq, but without relying on a single point of failure or control and all powered by open-source code. His trading world would be faster, safer, more open, and global. What could be better?

Samani was blown away.

Despite Lingham's high praise and a great couple of first calls, Samani came into the meeting with Yakovenko with relatively low expectations. He had read Yakovenko's white paper and was decidedly unimpressed. It was common for protocol developers to publish white papers that described their network and explained what made their blockchain unique. There was nothing distinctive or unique about Yakovenko's white paper. In fact, Samani remembered thinking it made no sense.

Initially, Solana was called Loom, a whimsical nod to how transactions were woven into the blockchain. The name Loom underscored the idea of woven threads, which is how Yakovenko and his other founders described how Solana's blockchain would incorporate multiple transactions to achieve its speed. Their blockchain would act as a virtual loom, weaving together various threads or transactions on a super-fast ledger. The problem was there was already another protocol called the Loom Network, which focused on gaming and social applications. To avoid confusion, Yakovenko and his founders decided to rebrand as Solana, an homage to the small coastal town just outside San Diego, California, where Yakovenko and some of the early founders used to surf and hang out. It lacked the philosophical references and poetic imagery that Loom conjured, but it was more personal and, in some ways, perhaps more practical. Solana was just a beautiful coastal town. Period. And that straightforward approach to naming the network echoed Yakovenko's approach to building it. He wasn't focused on the theoretical. Instead, he was obsessively focused on functionality. Many protocol founders only thought about scale and didn't pay enough attention to use cases. They would talk endlessly about decentralized trust in very abstract terms. Yakovenko was focused on the product. What could he build, and how could he service the user? That was his North Star. He wanted to create an on-chain marketplace, a digital and decentralized Nasdaq, and build the future of trading.

"I'm not interested in solving unsolvable math problems," Yakovenko told Samani. "I'm not an academic. I have little use for academics." They both chuckled at the comment as it recalled countless, pointless hours of theoretical discourse about some cryptographic system, consensus algorithm, or other super-fine technical points. Yakovenko had already tried that in his previous life as an engineer, first at chip giant Qualcomm and later working on various decentralized systems. He preferred instead to build on the work of others. He wasn't an academic and wasn't trying to solve unsolvable problems. He almost seemed to loathe academia, contrary to his peers. He wanted to build big, ambitious projects. He wanted to see results and use his knowledge of engineering to construct real, tangible systems that could bring about change. Global change. Change that could disrupt age-old systems. He wasn't just engineering a system; he was creating a new one. He was engineering opportunity.

Yakovenko was born in Ukraine and moved to Illinois at nine, with his family allowed just $50 each by the USSR. When he arrived, he expected to see Manhattan-style skyscrapers from coast to coast. Instead, he found cornfields and suburbia. At the University of Illinois, he studied computer science and earned a surprisingly mundane 3.2 GPA for a future crypto wizard. Mostly, he split his time between classes and underwater hockey, a niche sport where he and his buddies competed in world championships. "Half the qualification was affording the try-outs," he would tell friends.

Although he was young when he arrived in America, his upbringing in Ukraine had a profound impact on him. America was teeming with opportunity. State media controlled access to information in Soviet-ruled Ukraine. The government deter-mined what you saw and read. In many ways, challenging that system was just another unsolvable problem. The introduction to a free and open society immediately sparked a fire in young Yakovenko. He turned a teenager just as the Internet and dot-com boom started to take off, and he threw himself into com-puters, devouring anything he could about coding and computer science.

While some of his classmates dreamed of being the next Derek Jeter, he longed to be the next Bill Gates or Larry Ellison, the people whose software was giving birth to the Internet and reshaping the global economy. Those businesses were not just making money; they were changing the world and providing, at the touch of a button, the type of information that would've been banned back in his homeland. Ukraine in the 1990s was characterized by centralized government control, but the Internet had the power to change that. It would turn informa-tion into water, flowing freely through a series of pipes. The possibilities were endless.

Yakovenko's passion for tech was tested when the dot-com boom turned to a bust during his time in college. Advisors, friends, and even some professors urged him to shun the tech sector, but he stuck with it, eventually landing a job at Qualcomm, where he spent more than a decade designing global operating systems. It was an excellent fit for an ambitious engineer, and in Qualcomm, he found an environment where the best and hardest-working individuals were largely left to do their work. He often volunteered for the toughest assignments, partly because of the challenge but mainly because the managers tended to leave the most ambitious alone to marinate in their missions.

By 2017, Yakovenko was more into AI than crypto. He and a buddy, Steve Akridge, a fellow Qualcomm engineer and underwater hockey teammate who would later become a future Solana co-founder, were experimenting with graphic processing units (GPUs), attempting to optimize deep learning models. Deep learning was a precursor to what is now commonly called AI—computers that learn from large piles of data. Deep learning requires a bunch of GPUs, which are designed to accelerate the processing of images and are essential for deep learning because of their computing power and ability to do tons of computations super-fast. These GPUs were initially used to generate graphics (remember when Nvidia was a way to trade video games?) but are now used to power AI. GPUs weren't and still aren't cheap, so to pay for them, Yakovenko and Akridge mined crypto on the side. GPUs are the essential ingredient for solving highly complex computations in a relatively short period of time. They are the "super" that powers supercomputing.

What was effectively a side hustle to a side hustle sparked great curiosity in Yakovenko. He had always been aware of crypto but was more or less lukewarm to the space. He obviously knew and had heard of Bitcoin and its smart contract brethren Ethereum, but he didn't view either as the next iteration of global finance. In truth, it all seemed a bit early in the space to declare anything, and from the outside, crypto seemed like some sort of complex exercise in simple speculation. But as he learned more, he became increasingly curious. Soon, he realized that a quiet revolution was happening in crypto. For someone who had spent so much time building global networks, the promise of a decentralized computer that a central authority couldn't control was both exciting and personally inspiring. That promise represented the kind of future he could only dream of in Ukraine, and the new blockchain technology challenged his analytical mind in ways traditional computing did not. However, one problem he frequently addressed was how to scale the blockchain, specifically how to make it faster. That's when Yakovenko started poking around at the Bitcoin proof-of-work concept, asking why it was so frustratingly inefficient. Proof-of-work is what crypto engineers generally refer to as a consensus mechanism. It's the method Bitcoin and other cryptocurrencies use to agree on the state and order of events that occur on a blockchain. On decentralized and distributed ledgers, the network is maintained by a community of users who are constantly verifying information and transactions (more on this later) through solving a series of complicated math equations that result in block rewards. But it can be slow and at times expensive if the network is busy. But why, Yakovenko wondered, did Bitcoin need an army of GPUs to churn out a block every 10 minutes? Why were transactions so slow? And so expensive? Surely, he thought, there must be a better way.

The 2017 crypto boom, with prices spiking and startups raising millions, only heightened his curiosity. Something was happening, but he wasn't sure exactly what. Later that year, a eureka moment hit him one night at Cafe Soleil, a San Diego bar where Yakovenko and Akridge were nursing drinks and griping about the blockchain's flaws.

"Why do we need all these GPUs?" Yakovenko asked. "It's so wasteful, and it's so slow." The conversation veered to Ethereum, which Yakovenko dismissed as "JavaScript on Bitcoin—cute but sluggish." Then, at 4 a.m., wired on caffeine and frustration, a light bulb went off. After two coffees and a beer, a concept just popped into his head. Caffeine tended to make him jittery, and he found it difficult to code after drinking too many cups. He turned to Akridge, his eyebrows raised and mouth slightly ajar. He started slowly.

"What if you could encode time as a data structure?" Yakovenko asked Akridge. "Not entropy, like Bitcoin, but just the passage of time." And with this, the seed of proof of history, Solana's superpower, was born, and so began the genesis for an idea that would eventually become the Solana network, an open global network that would redefine the rules of financial technology.

What made the proof-of-history concept so radical is that it gave birth to the idea that the passage of time could be used to help order events on the blockchain. That concept would allow the Solana blockchain to operate at a much faster speed than Bitcoin or, most importantly, Ethereum, which specialized in programmable money. Ethereum was a great concept, but it had obvious flaws around speed and costs. Proof of history was the kind of idea that sounds obvious in hindsight but was radical in 2017. Bitcoin was a digital ledger that proved work through computational sweat; Yakovenko wanted to prove time. He wasn't thinking about building a company yet, just solving a puzzle that had been nagging him.

In its simplest terms, proof of history is like a built-in clock for the blockchain. Typically, blockchains like Bitcoin or Ethereum require all the computers or nodes to agree on the order of transactions through a series of constant and regular confirmations, which require even more time. With proof of history, the Solana protocol creates a historical record, almost like a virtual timestamp, proving when transactions happen without needing constant verification.

A simpler explanation might be to imagine a group of people all yelling simultaneously, trying to determine who spoke first. It would be chaotic and wildly unproductive to say nothing of being noisy, but eventually, there would be a consensus as to who spoke first. Now imagine filming that same group of people all yelling. Instead of debating who spoke first, you could simply go back to the video to see who spoke first. This is considerably faster than debating and is just as trustworthy as you can see on the tape who spoke first. Checking the videotape eliminates the need to focus on who spoke first since we can simply look at the video and see, well, who actually spoke first. As a result, we can focus on what was said instead of who said it first.

Proof of history imputes that concept onto the blockchain. The nodes can trust the order of events, and since that order has been firmly established, they can instead turn their focus to verifying the transaction, allowing for incredible speed and many more transactions. It dramatically reduces the time spent confirming the order of events, which enables the Solana network to handle way more transactions per second. In short, it's faster, which makes it the perfect system for payments or decentralized apps that require great speed at lower costs and is perfect for creating the marketplace of the next generation.

Yakovenko knew he had something, and he began to enlist help. He brought in fellow Qualcomm co-workers Greg Fitzgerals as well as particle physicist Eric Williams and Raj Gokal. Williams actually introduced Yakovenko to Gokal years before. Unlike the other co-founders, Gokal came from a tech healthcare startup, Omada Health, where he was director of product and Williams led data science. Williams was more the technologist while Gokal was more the marketing guy. They had become good friends, and one day Williams invited Gokal on a camping trip, where he first met Yakovenko.

"He was a cool guy. Obviously very brilliant, kind of nerdy, and it was clear he wanted to build," Gokal would later recall. When they met, he was struck by how focused and intense Yakovenko was, to the point where he would seem almost oblivious to what was happening outside his head. When they first met, Yakovenko would often stare off into the woods, likely contemplating some intense equation. The two got on great during the trip, and as Yakovenko talked about his work at Qualcomm, Gokal was struck by how passionate Yakovenko was about building great technology. He came off as someone who'd be a great business partner, obsessed with building great products, dedicated but with a quiet intensity that belied his ambition. Gokal made a quick mental note to keep him on his radar.

Gokal continued his work in health tech, but the space was beginning to frustrate him. To make a product that truly caught fire, you needed technology to have a disruptive effect, like how cell phones disrupted landlines or how Uber defined the market for mobility and rendered taxi medallions worthless. But between the insurance companies and the regulators, disrupting the tightly regulated healthcare industry proved nearly impossible. That vice-like grip on innovation was too much for Gokal, a young Wharton grad who was itching to use tech to carve out a new industry. So he began work on other tech projects. Around four years after that initial camping trip, Gokal caught up with his friend Williams over a drink in July 2017.

"Remember that guy Toly I introduced you to," asked Williams, using Yakovenko's nickname.

"Of course. The intense guy? Really smart. What's he up to?" Gokal asked, fondly recalling the time spent camping.

"He thinks he knows how to solve for scalability in block-chains. But he needs someone like you as a partner. I think you guys would work great together. You should talk to him and hear him out."

Gokal did not have an extensive background in cryptocurrency. His professional experience before Solana was primarily rooted in venture capital, product management, and health tech, with a focus on high-growth technology businesses rather than blockchain or crypto-specific endeavors. But he did have experience in traditional finance firms and was always looking for the next great disruptive technology. Early in his career, he worked as an analyst at KBW, a niche broker dealer and investment bank. Next was a hedge fund, Meridian Capital, before moving on to venture capital at General Catalyst Partners in Boston, where he scouted and analyzed investment opportunities in software systems and clean energy. Mostly though, his career was spent in the health-tech space. He co-founded Sano, a consumer medical device company before moving on to Omada Health.

In fact, prior to co-founding Solana Labs with Yakovenko, Gokal had little to actual no hands-on experience with blockchains or crypto projects, but what he did have was a considerable amount of expertise in scaling businesses, managing products, and navigating new and potentially disruptive fields, all skills that would serve him well. More interestingly, Gokal actually had real concerns over whether crypto would ever reach mainstream status and become a viable alternative to the existing traditional financial system. To him, the very early crypto products seemed niche, a better fit for thousands of technically savvy people rather than millions of users. How big could this crypto thing really get? Gokal couldn't see the value beyond simple speculation, which had a limited shelf life in his view. Still, the prospect of working with Yakovenko persuaded him to keep an open mind, and the two began to have regular coffee sessions.

What initially struck Gokal was that Yakovenko also appeared to harbor the same skepticism and concerns about the whole space.

"I don't know if this thing is going to change the world," Yakovenko told Gokal over lunch one day. "But if it is, it needs to be thousands of times faster and thousands of times more cost-effective with much lower latency than how Bitcoin or Ethereum are currently architected." That comment struck Gokal as rather interesting and, frankly, refreshing. Most crypto engineers, particularly L1 developers, tended to make bold claims and would tout their product's ability to change the existing financial world.

"It will supplant banking as we know it!" Some would claim.

"It will revolutionize the payment system!"

In truth, like many startups, most level-ones fail and fail miserably, burn cash, and scorch egos in the process. The birth of any industry has always been an existential fight to the finish, a brutal winner-take-all battle that pits ambition and perseverance against luck and untold wealth. At stake? Control, not just of an industry but of the future. Railroads. Banks. Steel. Autos. All built on the towering ambitions of people who asked not "why?" but "why not?" Most don't make it, and to the winner goes untold wealth. To the loser goes a wealth of pain.

At the turn of the twentieth century, there were more than 200 auto makers all vying to control the market. By 1920, that number shrunk to 25. Now there are just three domestic US-owned automakers. A hundred years ago, there were multiple studios and television stations. They have all since merged or gone out of business, leaving just a handful of conglomerates. Remember how many smartphone makers existed in the late 90s? Nokia, Palm, Ericsson, BlackBerry. You get the picture. Yakovenko, unlike other crypto engineers, was acutely aware of the challenges he faced, and he knew, or at least thought he knew, how to solve them.

"I've done the math," he told Gokal. "Bitcoin and Ethereum would top out if the entire population of Berkeley used both three times a day." It was a remarkable comment that laid bare some of the challenges facing the nascent crypto industry. What Yakovenko was saying was profound. By his work, the Bitcoin and Ethereum networks had only enough capacity to support the population of Berkeley, California, if all those people, just shy of 120,000, decided to use Bitcoin or Ethereum three times a day.

"If the vision for crypto is to have a vast, decentralized payment network that everyday people can log on and have decentralized finance, and your capacity is capped to the population of Berkeley. . .," Yakovenko trailed off. The point was clear. If this crypto thing was really going to become a thing, it needed to be faster, cheaper, and way more scalable.

Yakovenko identified another problem, too. In his view, the industry's general approach to scaling was just some form of sharding, which, based on his work in distributed systems at Qualcomm, was just wrong. In crypto, sharding is like splitting a big database into smaller, more manageable pieces called "shards." Each shard handles a portion of the workload, making the system faster and more efficient. It's basically just breaking up the work.

An even simpler analogy that most parents could probably understand is to imagine a huge box of toys that's so full it takes your kid forever to find anything. Now imagine that same box of toys had a computer that could keep track of who owns what and where it was stored without ever needing an adult to watch over it. Sharding is like splitting that big toy box into smaller boxes, with each one having some toys so you can search faster since they're not all jumbled together. In crypto, sharding splits up the work of keeping track of everything, allowing for greater speed in times of heavy use.

Ethereum relies heavily on sharding. Extending our analogy further, Ethereum is like a super-popular crypto toy box where people trade digital money and make things like games or art. But when too many people play with it at once, it gets crowded and sluggish. The pace of play slows down due to a lack of space. Sharding is a big deal for Ethereum because it makes everything faster so more people can use it. Yakovenko wanted to move away from this approach to something that could instantly tell you where a toy was and to whom it belonged, without the fuss of creating multiple boxes.

For Solana, sharding isn't directly used in its core design; however, the concept is relevant because Solana aims to solve the same problem: scaling a blockchain to handle a large number of transactions quickly. But instead of relying on it, Yakovenko chose to create proof of history and parallel processing to create greater speed. People compare parallel processing to sharding because both approaches address the challenge of maintaining a blockchain's speed and decentralization as it grows.

"The thinking of 'Let's just launch multiple chains and make them interoperable and talk to each other' just, like, won't work," Yakovenko said to Gokal in a sarcastic voice.

In short, Yakovenko wasn't interested in making a toy box with multiple boxes inside. He wanted something new and

different, radically different. His approach initially took the
Solana team by surprise, and early developers felt they were living in some version of *The Imitation Game*, the 2014 film about
the British mathematician Alan Turing. The film detailed Turing's
work cracking secret Nazi codes using a machine that could
decipher complex algorithms. Turing felt that a machine could
mimic human intelligence, a thought that seemed almost fantastical at the time and wasn't universally shared among his colleagues. To the early engineers on Solana, what Yakovenko was
trying to accomplish was just as wild and fantastical. The film
became a quiet source of inspiration for the team, almost a silent
nod to the Herculean effort they collectively embraced. Of
course, everyone was a believer in what Yakovenko was trying to
do. How could they not? His singular brilliance was a palpable
source of inspiration. However, the first couple of years of long
nights were more than just an endurance test; they were a test of
their resolve, a grueling challenge to change the new financial
order. They were pioneers, explorers in the truest sense, in this
new, vast digital world of blockchains and possibilities. Yakovenko
wasn't basing his approach on some of the other established
white papers at the time, like Cardano or Avalanche, projects
that had raised tens of millions of dollars and investors saw as the
best alternatives to finding true scaling solutions outside of
Ethereum; he was building from scratch. Many of the same
investors who committed to those other projects turned their
noses at the upstart Solana. The crypto intelligentsia who
invested in Cardano and the like didn't think much of Solana at
the time. They considered it too ambitious, too radical, and significantly underfunded to make a meaningful impact. It probably didn't help that Yakovenko's white paper was at best
perfunctory, at worst simplistic. But that wasn't surprising if you
knew Yakovenko at all. He had always thought white papers
were somewhat pointless, almost performative documents. He
was a doer, not a talker. He didn't spend hours explaining every
aspect of how the network would work, unlike other ambitious

level-one white papers. He wrote enough to speak to other seasoned engineers and have them understand the approach. That's all he needed. Action! Efficiency! If I have to explain it twice, you won't get it the third time. Let's move! Explaining every detail of how the entire system would work was pointless. He essentially wrote enough to gain buy-in and then focused on raising money, hiring, and building the product. It was classic Yakovenko; he'd rather work the problem than explain it to people.

To the crypto crowd, Yakovenko's pitch sounded like pure fantasy with a dash of delusion on the side. Bitcoin's white paper, the unofficial blockchain bible, states that you can't have a source of time without consensus. It's the first principle, the crypto equivalent of the First Commandment. Yakovenko was challenging that notion and taking a radically different tack, going all in on a decentralized source of time that offered a clarifying passage of events that would turbocharge the network. To pull it off, he'd have to gut the very idea of how blockchains functioned. To put it in simpler terms, he was creating the auto equivalent of a Tesla, a radically different vehicle whose only common characteristic with other cars was that it had four wheels and a steering wheel. Everything else was entirely different.

And that was just one of many other hurdles. In fact, for the engineers at Solana to be successful, they'd have to solve for speed, interoperability, usability, low transaction costs, accessibility, and a million other hurdles. It was not for the faint of heart, but they managed, and his vision prevailed in a blockchain that was faster, cheaper, and more scalable than anything that had come before.

He would need investors to help fund his vision, and in Samani, he found the perfect partner. Samani knew instantly that he was holding the coin equivalent of a winning lottery ticket. Solana solved for all of Ethereum's deficiencies and presented new opportunities that hadn't even been considered. It fit perfectly within Multicoin Capital's strategy for crypto investing.

They weren't playing the markets, buying this coin or that; they were making concentrated bets on the future, making all-in investments in the companies and businesses that would come to redefine future blockchains. They weren't just token pickers; they were picking crypto's future, looking for and doubling down on the next great thematic trade, and investing in the coin-equivalent of the next great Apple, even if that particular analogy irked him.

"Reasoning by analogy actively leads to the wrong conclusion," Samani would often tell clients who likened buying crypto to Apple or Google. Samani would smirk at those who tried to wedge crypto narratives into more familiar ones involving IBM and Apple. Those were short-sighted and, in his view, irrelevant comparisons. Samani preferred to frame Solana's attributes in terms of the future, and in Solana he saw a solution to all of Ethereum's problems.

"Ethereum will always be my first love. It got me into crypto," Samani would tell clients. "But they never committed to figuring out how to scale. Instead, they just relied on a series of layer 2s. They always took the wrong approach." Samani's point was a bit technical, but it underscored Solana's superiority, or Ethereum inferiority, depending on your perspective. Ethereum's network was so clunky and congested that it often relied on what is referred to as layer 2s. In crypto parlance, layer 2 solutions on Ethereum are protocols, or sets of rules, built on top of the Ethereum blockchain. The goal of layer 2s is to reduce costs and increase speed. This may sound complicated, but the concept is quite simple. In its most basic form, a layer 2 is simply additional space, much like an extra lane that relieves congestion.

In simplest terms, imagine a playground at recess. The kids rush out to the field to play basketball, football, tag, or jump rope. Eventually, there are too many kids in the playground, and the games begin to collide. The footballs end up on the basketball court, and an errant pitch stops play on the football field. In short, it's chaos. To alleviate this congestion, the teachers decide to open an adjacent, connecting field. Now the kids can play freely without having to wait for one game to conclude. Everything is smooth. That adjacent field is like building a layer 2 in crypto; it alleviates congestion and makes things move faster, particularly when there are many people on the network.

This is a crude but unfortunately fitting analogy to describe the Ethereum blockchain when it gets busy; too many people trading NFTs or lending virtual money eventually clog the system. The Ethereum blockchain is like that giant playground with millions of children playing games and trading objects. Instead of trading toys and playing basketball, they're trading digital toys and playing virtual games. And every time one of those kids decides to do something, they have to write it down in a notebook to make sure everyone agrees it happened. Extending this further, imagine if every time a kid played a game, they had to pay a small fee to the teachers, particularly when it got crowded. That's precisely what happens in Ethereum; users are often forced to pay "gas fees" to alleviate all the congestion.

To fix or avoid all this hassle, engineers build what is called layer 2s. Now, instead of everyone crowding into one field, they can spill over into two, where there is much more room for activity, reducing gas fees and making things move faster. The layer 2 solution enables transactions to be processed off-chain (in the adjacent field) while remaining connected to the Ethereum blockchain (in the main field). This enables faster and more cost-effective transactions. Everything is still recorded onto the Ethereum blockchain, but it's just moving faster.

Now this may sound like a great solution, but it's not. Ethereum requires layer 2s because it can process only a limited number of transactions at once. It needs to, in essence, relocate the work from the main playground to an alternative one. The two playgrounds are connected, so all the activity is recorded and monitored by the teachers, which you can think of as nodes, but it's a chaotic and expensive process. Why does Ethereum do this? Why not just build a bigger playground? It's undoubtedly a question Samani had asked many times before.

The simple answer is that Ethereum designers want to keep the blockchain safe. Sticking with the playground analogy, they want to ensure the kids don't get hurt and can track everyone's movement. Using a layer 2 allows for better tracking of transactions; the teachers can keep a better eye on the kids if they're spread across two fields as opposed to one, and they can still play at the same speeds. Samani disliked this approach and considered it woefully antiquated. Why not simply build a different kind of playground?

Solana was that different playground, bigger, sleeker, and built to handle multiple games at once. Instead of having adjacent fields to handle extra kids, Solana's playground has slides that instantly transport them, all while keeping everyone safe. And since there is no line and no crowding, no one has to pay fees to the teacher. In short, it's the playground of the future where lines are short, everyone is running around, but they're all still safe. And as such, Solana doesn't need layer 2s. Its layer 2 is embedded in its system through proof of history and parallel processing. Now, to be clear, there are network extensions, which effectively act as a layer 2, but speed is integrated into the blockchain's protocol. In the case of Solana, there is no need to create an adjacent playground, as all the kids can play safely and quickly on the main one. Solana's blockchain is a one-stop shop destination where all transactions can happen on the main network.

Now, I know this all sounds like a lot. It certainly was for me when I first entered the world of the coin. When I first heard about Bitcoin and the blockchain, I dismissed much of it as mathematical gymnastics. Fortunately, I surrounded myself with coin-curious colleagues who pushed me to understand this fast-growing and exciting world better. I don't know where I'd be personally or professionally had I not had that good fortune. Still, as a Wall Street professional of 30 years, embracing crypto required more than just a suspension of disbelief. But it's essential to take a moment and understand the concepts behind Bitcoin and the blockchain if you want to understand why Solana and other crypto investments can be disruptive.

Bitcoin's original white paper, supposedly authored by Satoshi Nakamoto in 2008, outlined a revolutionary concept that changed money forever and gave birth to the modern crypto world that we now know. It birthed the idea of the popular understanding of the digital token or coin and the idea of the blockchain and mining. It proposed a radical concept of exchanging value between two parties without using a bank or government entity. Digital money has existed since the word "digital" was invented, but early concepts of digital money existed in closed end-to-end systems. Think of products like DigiCash or ECash in the early 90s. Those products were centralized. Bitcoin and the blockchain were decentralized, meaning the responsibility to maintain the network was distributed among its users. The blockchain was composed of parties who were both users of the network and custodians of it.

Best of all, Bitcoin would be incorruptible. No central bank or government could debase it by printing more because no central bank or government would ruin it. It existed outside the boundaries of traditional financial systems. It belonged to the people, even if it didn't belong to a specific group or governing body. In an age of excess money printing, Bitcoin and the blockchain on which it operated represented financial purity. Best of all, it was portable. You could transport billions of it instantly. You could carry it in a thumb drive and transport it in the palm of your pocket. Bitcoin dwarfed any alleged advantage gold claimed to offer. It was a digital store of value. Better still, it was digital property.

Bitcoin transactions would be recorded on a digital distributed ledger called a "blockchain." All you needed to participate was an Internet connection and copious computing power to verify all the transactions. Users with access to special equipment could "mine" Bitcoin by solving complicated math equations and be rewarded for their work with actual bitcoins. Mining Bitcoin was modeled after the gold mining process and was designed to get harder over time. Only 21 million bitcoins could ever be mined. Miners maintain the trust and integrity of the blockchain by completing these increasingly complicated math problems. Nakamoto's paper decreed that anyone who could verify one megabyte of Bitcoin would be rewarded with a part of a coin. Miners represent the shared trust essential to maintaining the Bitcoin ecosystem and upholding the legitimacy of each Bitcoin transaction. Single transactions are grouped into individual blocks and then added to a chain of blocks to form the actual blockchain. To confirm a single block, a miner must solve a series of math problems, specifically, a 64-digit hexadecimal number called a hash. This process of validating transactions is called "proof of work." I like to think of it as a synchronized virtuous cycle where the blockchain is maintained by miners, who are, in turn, rewarded with tokens for their work.

This is a lot to take in, and I can hear the cynics screaming. I know this because I used to be one of them. I grew up a working-class kid from Long Island in the 1960s, so I'm hard-wired to smell BS or worse. But if you take a moment, you'll realize that blockchains already exist in many forms in our economy.

I like to think of blockchains as businesses. If blockchains offer excellent service and efficiency, customers will enjoy and want to use them, just like businesses. But to access this business and avail yourself of all its natural advantages, you'll need to purchase and use its native tokens or coins. This concept already exists, and you've likely participated in it. When you go to a casino, you exchange your dollars for chips, which are used to access the poker and blackjack tables. Those casino chips function just like coins or tokens; they allow you access to the economy of the casino. They allow you to gamble and can even be used to purchase drinks, maybe many! However, they will also enable the casino to operate more efficiently. Chips minimize theft and fraud as they can only be used in the casino. For example, a gambler on a cold streak might be tempted to grab his cash and dash for the exits. Running off with the chips would prove worthless since they are only good inside the casino. He would have to take the chips and exchange them back into cash to access his money. Using chips also mini-mizes the threat of someone trying to gamble with counterfeit money since all bills are checked for authenticity when gamblers exchange their cash. In this example, using the chips enhances eve-ryone's safety and makes the casino more efficient. Customers enter the casino, exchange their fiat dollars for chips, and use these chips to access the casino's economy efficiently. At each step, the process of changing dollars into chips, gambling, and then chang-ing those chips back into dollars is verified and authenticated at each step.

This is no different than changing your dollars into a specific cryptocurrency to access the efficiency of a particular blockchain. For those who believe in the future of on-chain businesses, the goal is to eventually use the native token of a blockchain, elimi-nating the need to toggle between fiat and cryptocurrencies. You may think this is far off, but your kids likely don't. That's because they are already doing it. When I grew up, money was tangible. You did something and were rewarded with a certain amount of physical money. Taking out the trash? That was worth a quarter. My paper route? Five dollars, and in my last year, it increased to 10, mainly due to my ability to get people to sign up for addi-tional subscriptions. But kids today are different. They don't use paper money even though they spend a lot of it. A Federal Reserve payment study estimated that 46% of all transactions involved physical cash in 2003. By 2023, the number had fallen to just 18%. As Yogi Berra might say, "A nickel ain't worth a dime anymore."

Ask a 10-year-old how much a car might cost, and you'll likely be met with a blank stare. Ask them what a slice of pizza costs, and you'll likely be met with that same stare. But ask them what a Cleanrot Knight's Sword on *Elden Ring* costs, and they can tell you down to the decimal how much it costs in Runes, which are that game's native currency. What if your child plays *Fortnite*? That requires V-Bucks, which can be used to purchase various virtual items. You may not recognize V-Bucks or Runes by name, but you've likely seen their footprint on your credit card bill. That would be the recurring charge of $9.99 per month. Get the picture? These virtual currencies allow your children to access the economies of their digital world more efficiently.

I often ask, what if Jeff Bezos said one day, "Hey, if you want to continue to use Amazon Prime, you can't use dollars. You have to use an Amazon coin"? Chances are, 98% of you would jump at the opportunity, and why not? Amazon's economy makes life easier. You can buy groceries. Movies. Clothes. Anything, and it arrives in 24 hours. What could be better? There's a reason the company is worth $2 trillion.

Now, Bezos says, "The coin is going to cost 1 cent." So, each Amazon buck costs you a dollar and a cent. Nobody would bat an eye. A penny for all that convenience? I'm willing to bet that people would continue to pay up to use these imaginary Amazon coins until they hit about 10 cents for every dollar, at which point the cost of convenience runs head first into the benefits of the frictionless Amazon economy. If you open your mind to that concept, then you can begin to understand the world of blockchains and coins.

Coins are just the tools to access the economies of various blockchains. Some businesses are more serious and understandable than others, but a lot of that depends on your perspective. A Taylor Swift coin may sound ridiculous to you. But what if 1,000 Taylor coins, let's call them Swfcoins (Taylor, you have to perform at the next SALT conference if you use this idea), enables you to see her tweets before anyone else? What if her coins gave you early access to tickets at one of her concerts or if Swfcoins allowed you to buy her merch at a discount? You may pass, but your 12-year-old daughter would buy it hand over fist. As more and more Swifties exchanged their fiat dollars for Swfcoins, the Taylor Swift blockchain would continue to grow and mature. It would become its own economy, powered by its coin. Don't tell me that's not a utility. What if Swfcoins could be used to purchase exclusive access to Taylor herself? I think you get the picture, and while this may sound a little out there, I don't believe that day is too far out.

You might ask, why not simply use dollars to buy those things? The answer is simple: you can't access this type of world using fiat because it would involve securities laws and the fiat banking system. That is not a fun place kids want to access. A Swfcoin stays out of the banking system and lives in a digitally-native setting that kids like to play in. Kids don't like banks and regulation; neither do adults if we are being intellectually honest. I'm not saying this is going to replace the modern financial system. True believers thought Bitcoin would do that. However, replacing the banks was not what Bitcoin was really about. It was about Bitcoin assimilating into the financial system through exchange-traded funds (ETFs) or other products. At some point, whether it's Taylor Swift or another superstar celebrity or athlete, someone will figure out how to imbue their fame into a fun, fast, and enjoyable financial ecosystem. So, if you are asking me if there is a real future in some of these coins. Absolutely, and Solana is the network that will power them.

This leads to an important aspect of understanding the world of the coin. Different blockchains aren't necessarily better than others, but they are better for certain types of activities. For example, Bitcoin is likely the best global store of value, in part because its blockchain is highly secure and safe. However, it's not ideal for creating smart contracts that can offer users programmable money. The Ethereum blockchain is a superior network for handling those types of transactions. But, it's not perfect. It can be slow and at times expensive, as we have detailed earlier. For me, Solana is the superior network for creating decentralized applications and tokenizing assets (much more on that later). One network isn't necessarily better than the other. They're just better for different things.

I'll break it down in simpler terms. Would you go to a four-star restaurant if you're famished and wanted a quick meal? Of course not. The wait alone would drive you crazy. You'd want something fast, tasty, and perhaps even affordable. In these moments, Shake Shack might do the trick. Is Shake Shack better than a four-star restaurant like New York City's The Grill? Of course not, but in certain situations it could be. Conversely, if you want to celebrate a special occasion like a birthday or graduation, you'd like to mark the occasion by going to a longer, multicourse meal at a fancy place like The Grill. And then there are times when perhaps you'd want something in the middle, a neighborhood restaurant that serves quality food but doesn't require three hours and a second mortgage. There are times in your life when each would be more preferable, and that's not a qualitative statement. It's just a fact. Bitcoin is a long, drawn-out fancy meal. Ethereum is the neighborhood restaurant, and Solana is Shake Shack. Each is delicious and appropriate for different situations; it's just a matter of what your needs and preferences are. One is not "better" than the other, but each is better for different needs. Solana, with its combination of speed, scale, and cost, represents the best investment and likely the best blockchain to access and profit from crypto's future. And that's what drew Samani to Solana.

He and his partners at Multicoin Capital needed a blockchain that could process transactions quickly and cheaply, dirt cheaply. That was the only way to realize Yakovenko's vision for a virtual marketplace—an on-chain order book that could accommodate millions of complex financial transactions in seconds for pennies. Solana could be the foundation of a new digital, global marketplace of the future. How on Earth could you build an on-chain Nasdaq on Ethereum? With all the layer 2s, you would need like a 100 mini Nasdaqs inside of the Nasdaq. Solana was perfect!

"The layer 2 roadmap for Ethereum was the fundamental wrong approach," Samani would tell investors. "Having so many layer 2s breaks composability," he added. Composability in crypto is a key concept. Generally speaking, it refers to the interoperability of different blockchains, allowing decentralized apps to work together. In other words, it allows one set of protocols to work with another.

A simple analogy might be how your Roku interacts with your streaming devices on your smart TV. Having layer 2s L2s degrades overall interoperability. In such an environment, it is impossible to have near-instant trading.

"Our vision was a global order book and a single global system that can support trading in any asset from around the world in real time with the best liquidity and best vision for crypto," Samani would tell clients. "This is the future of global financial markets. And that future is just not on the Ethereum network."

Samani left San Francisco convinced he had found his guy. He returned to his Multicoin Capital co-founder, Tushar Jain, to discuss a potential investment. Samani was convinced that Yakovenko's approach and goal were right. It was time to put their money where their mouths were. So, in 2018, Samani and his partners made a series of concentrated Solana-centric bets. They led one seed round for a $20 million investment in Solana as part of Series A funding. They led another round in the summer of 2019 and yet another in early 2020, when the blockchain was launched. Additionally, they purchased SOL tokens, the native currency of the Solana blockchain. They weren't just doubling down. They were all in.

It was just the start.

Chapter 4

The Call

"Nice to see you, Sam. Can everyone hear okay?" Kyle Samani asked.

It was 11 p.m. in Texas, where Samani was living, 9 p.m. in California, where Anatoly Yakovenko was logged in, and just past noon in Hong Kong, when Sam Bankman-Fried (SBF) logged on to the call to discuss a relatively new blockchain called Solana. The call was scheduled for 30 minutes. It lasted nearly three hours.

It was July 7, 2020, and the world was in an unprecedented global lockdown. Solana tokens, which had just launched three months before, were worth just shy of a dollar, but that would soon change. A new phenomenon was gripping the crypto markets. Ethereum's DeFi Summer was about to take hold, a speculative orgy that would see Ether and many other popular coins surge in value. DeFi is short for "decentralized finance," referring to financial applications built on blockchain technology that enable users to borrow, lend, trade, or earn interest on their cryptocurrency (more on this later), all outside the traditional banks and financial intermediaries that comprise the TradFi landscape. Different DeFi projects were seemingly launched daily. New terms like "staking" and "yield farming" became standard vernacular on CNBC and broader financial media.

When investors stake their cryptocurrency, they pledge or lend it to a blockchain network in exchange for rewards. Staking supports the network by validating transactions and securing the blockchain. In return, you earn coins as a reward. The process is similar to depositing money in a bank and earning interest, but in this case, there is no bank, and the reward comes in the form of extra coins instead of interest. Yield farming is similar, but it is generally used to lend coins to DeFi apps to provide liquidity. This is usually riskier and, as a result, offers higher returns in the form of more tokens. Investors often chase the best rates among different platforms, swapping out one coin for another. If staking is like depositing money at a bank, yield farming can be likened to trading options, offering better returns but at the cost of taking more significant risks.

The Defi Summer of 2020 laid bare the promise and pitfalls of a new and exciting decentralized world. Cartoon-like virtual apes, nonfungible tokens (NFTs, effectively digital trading cards), and new apps popped up seemingly every day. The once-unimaginable virtual world of the coin was materializing before our eyes, on our phones and laptops, minting millionaires who were all too happy to point a finger at the stodgy old guard. Wealth wasn't just celebrated; it was flaunted on Twitter and Instagram. Speculative investments like SPACs (blank check companies that allowed companies to go public faster) and NFTs vied for investors' attention as government stimulus checks, or "stimmys," were quickly converted into digital coins. And Ethereum was at the center of it all. Several DeFi platforms, such as Compound and Yearn, were built on the Ethereum blockchain, and their high yields provided a nice alternative to the ultra-low interest rates found in traditional financial markets. But if the moment shined a light on Ethereum's promise, it also seared a harsh spotlight on its pitfalls. Its slow speed and staggering costs were frequent topics on Reddit threads and chat rooms. The frustration was palpable; the desire for an alternative was even greater.

Of course, with booms come busts, and many of these risky programs collapsed under the weight of their speculative behavior. Investors, perhaps unaware of the risks, lost a substantial amount of money. Others cashed in on the relatively unregulated market; either way, a mania was afoot. However, the interesting thing about booms and busts is that they often accompany periods of great innovation. The dot-com bubble of 2000 wiped out trillions, but it also gave birth to the modern Internet, which has since led to even greater prosperity. That was true in 2020. Lost in the panoply of Apes, Memes, lending apps, and soaring coin prices was the beginning of a lasting and substantive foundation that would lead to even greater crypto prosperity. The wild speculation proved the rocket fuel for even wilder growth, a virtual decentralized world where anyone could access prosperity. It was glorious. It was frightening. It was capitalism at its best, and worst.

During the peak of the cryptocurrency boom, one company and one individual stole the spotlight. FTX, a cryptocurrency exchange founded by SBF just a year before, emerged as a transformative force in the digital asset industry. Headquartered in the Bahamas, FTX rapidly evolved from a fledgling startup to a major player in the global crypto market. The exchange facilitated trading in thousands of cryptocurrencies, offering both spot and derivatives markets, as well as its proprietary token, FTT. With its blend of technology and design, FTX made trading cryptocurrency fun and intuitive. In short order, FTX attracted millions of users, ranking as the third-largest crypto exchange by trading volume, trailing only Binance and Coinbase. Its growth was fueled by an impressive roster of investors, including a who's who of financial royalty, such as BlackRock, Sequoia, and SoftBank's Masayoshi Son, to name a few. In a remarkably short time, FTX achieved what takes most companies decades: it built a globally recognized brand, and not just any brand, but one that screamed legitimacy. In the world of virtual currencies, reputation was the most valuable asset, and FTX built a great one. It was more than just an exchange; it was a cultural phenomenon. The FTX logo appeared on stadiums, billboards, and television screens during NBA games. High-profile endorsements from celebrities and athletes propelled the exchange's visibility. It was a household name, alongside the likes of Bank of America. Even if you had no idea what it did, you knew the name or had seen one of their commercials during a sporting event.

At the core of FTX's success was SBF, who was different from the rest of the crypto crowd. He eschewed Lambos and flashy jewelry, choosing instead to wrap himself in wrinkled T-shirts and crumpled, oversized cargo shorts. Don't get me wrong. SBF knew how to live, but his lifestyle reminded me of the character from the movie *Big*, the classic Tom Hanks film about a child trapped in an adult's body. He owned a palatial $40 million apartment in the Bahamas. Still, it was sparsely furnished and looked like an expensive college dorm, which it sort of was, with its rotating cast of friends and coders coming and going and living in various rooms. Video games were strewn about next to hot tubs. Maids came every day, but the place was still a mess.

He was a frenetic mass of intellect and energy, his hair shooting up in the air, less a style than a middle finger to gravity. His dark, pitch-black eyes almost seemed to flicker when he blinked, like a screen that was loading improperly, and they were constantly in motion, furiously darting around in what seemed like a desperate attempt to keep up with his continually vibrating knee. He was born in Palo Alto, California, in 1992 and grew up in a well-educated, upper-middle-class Jewish family. His parents, Joseph Bankman and Barbara Fried, were Stanford Law School professors, upstanding individuals of principle. SBF and his younger brother, Gabe, grew up around dinner tables filled with food and heady debates. They talked about inequality, justice, and debated principles of fairness, all topics that would later inform SBF's philosophy of effective altruism. It wasn't just talk. It was the early code that programmed SBF's worldview.

He was a quiet kid. Autism spectrum disorder shaped his world. Social cues were a frustrating mystery. One moment, he could decipher incredibly complex mathematical patterns and, in the next, be bewildered entirely by a casual glance. He'd fake smiles to get along. He didn't have many friends in Crystal Springs Uplands, a tony, elite private school. Primarily, he spent a lot of time playing video games. But he was an extraordinary student. School work was almost too easy. He'd spend his summers at Math Camp just to feel stimulated. After high school, it was off to MIT, the high church of mathematics, but even that was too easy for him. Classes felt like a waste. He'd often skip them to spend time with his frat brothers at Epsilon Theta, a math-focused fraternity. There was some beer pong, but mainly it was late-night coding sessions and computer games.

After MIT, SBF jumped into trading at Jane Street Capital in 2014, the Wall Street quant firm, where he'd spend his days looking for tiny price discrepancies others could not see. Finally, a puzzle that could engage him, even stump him at times. He'd stare at his screen for hours straight, processing millions of little pieces of data like a human calculator. He'd go head-to-head against the computers, like one of the many video games from his childhood, and he'd crush it, acing another math problem without breaking a sweat. It was like solving a puzzle for money, but the pay was big.

It was in 2017 at Jane Street that SBF spotted a massive opportunity. Huge price discrepancies across various crypto exchanges were creating what every trader prays for each morning: an arbitrage opportunity. Prices for Bitcoin and other coins varied wildly across global exchanges. You could buy, for example, one Bitcoin for $10,000 on one exchange and sell it for $11,000 on another. The $1,000 difference was pure profit. For a savvy trader, this was like mainlining heroin. It was too good to be true, like shooting virtual fish in a barrel. But you had to be fast, really fast, and you had to see the opportunity before anyone else. SBF couldn't look a cyclops in the eye if his life depended on it, but he sure could spot a trade. The only way to make money was to see it first. SBF saw everything first.

"That's the lowest hanging fruit," SBF would later tell CNBC. In particular, he noticed Bitcoin prices in South Korea were really out of whack. He called it the "Kimchi Premium," a nod to the Korean delicacy of sour, fermented cabbage. The cabbage was sour, but the profits were sweet. Realizing he was sitting on a pot of virtual gold, he left Jane Street in 2018 to found Alameda Research, a crypto trading firm named after the town in which he was living when he started the company. Alameda capitalized on these market inefficiencies, generating millions in profits and transforming SBF into a multimillionaire virtually overnight. This success laid the foundation for FTX, which he launched a year later, leveraging Alameda's profits and expertise to create an exchange that would redefine the industry.

SBF's wealth grew exponentially as FTX rose. By 2021, *Forbes* estimated his net worth at $22.5 billion, making him one of the wealthiest individuals in the world, all before his 30th birthday. And he funneled much of that money into philanthropy, guided by the principles of effective altruism, which was a philosophy that could best be likened to charity on steroids. SBF joined the Giving Pledge, alongside billionaires like Bill Gates. He established the FTX Foundation, which allocated 1% of the exchange's revenue to charitable causes, including global health, poverty alleviation, climate change, and other related issues. By 2022, he had donated hundreds of millions of dollars and had become the leading philanthropist in the crypto space. He wasn't a political figure, but his contributions supported hot-button and left-leaning issues, such as global warming. He was refashioning charity for the new age; he was young, rich, and generous. He was a socially conscious billionaire who intended to use his wealth for the greater good. He was Bill Gates 2.0, the crypto version, younger and more approachable. He became a regular on financial media and, before long, a cultural figure in America. Banking CEOs sought him out. Politicians, many of whom were on the receiving end of SBF's generosity, cozied up to him. Models and celebrities flocked to him.

And he was a master marketer.

Sure, FTX had great technology and innovation. The platform was fun and welcoming to beginners. But SBF's other superpower was his marketing savvy. He understood that building a brand required more than a reliable platform; it demanded visibility and trust. Could you trust your trade would go through? Could you trust that your money was safe? FTX's marketing strategy was aggressive and far-reaching, designed to capture the attention of both crypto enthusiasts and Bitcoin beginners. The company secured naming rights for the Miami Heat's arena, rebranded as the FTX Arena, and sponsored events ranging from Formula 1 races to eSports tournaments. Its advertisements, one hilarious one featured Larry David as a skeptic dismissing crypto and FTX itself, ran during the Super Bowl, and it was just the start. FTX ads were everywhere, making FTX a recognizable name beyond the crypto community. Celebrity endorsements poured in. Tom Brady, a seven-time Super Bowl champion, not only endorsed FTX but also took an equity stake in the company. NBA great Stephen Curry signed on as a global ambassador, while supermodel Gisele Bündchen, Brady's then-wife, joined the FTX Foundation's advisory board. A hot product only got hotter, fueled by an intoxicating mix of celebrity, wealth, technology, and innovation. And there was perhaps no bigger personality than SBF himself.

He became a ubiquitous figure, his presence felt across media platforms and public forums. He was a frequent guest on cable news networks, including CNBC, CNN, Fox, and Bloomberg, where he discussed cryptocurrency markets, trading strategies, and social issues. He hit the podcast circuit, where clips would ricochet around Instagram and YouTube. He'd break down classic crypto concepts with the same effortless ease of a professional basketball player dunking a ball, and he'd often do it while multi-tasking on his computer, tending to a trade, or spotting some market dislocation, all while being live on TV! He hit the global thought-leader circuits, becoming a regular at industry confer-ences, the World Economic Forum in Davos, and crypto summits in Dubai, where he spoke on panels about regulation, innovation, and philanthropy. His X account was a constant stream of insights, ranging from market analysis to thoughts on effective altruism. Traders hung on his every post. He was the subject of in-depth profiles in the *New York Times* and *Forbes*, each portraying him as a quirky genius reshaping the financial world. They'd often point out his preference for socks and sandals, noting how his lack of polish stood in contrast to the established TradFi banking brethren at Goldman or Morgan Stanley. He dressed as kids imagined they would if one day they, too, had a billion dollars. However, his unique style wasn't a result of his lack of taste. He could care less about that. It was something more profound. The crumpled shirts, baggy shorts and sloppy sandals weren't a fashion statement; they were props, mini megaphones that allowed him to silently scream a message for all to hear: I have F-you money and you don't!

FTX's partnerships extended beyond sports to gaming and entertainment, tapping into younger folks who saw crypto as cool and fun. This omnipresence was no accident, and the intent of the message was clear: FTX was synonymous with cryptocur-rency itself; it was the asset class. By 2021, FTX was processing billions of dollars in daily trading volume, cementing its status as a cornerstone of the crypto ecosystem, and SBF's brand was a critical component of the company's success. His carefully culti-vated image of authenticity, intelligence, and social awkwardness connected with the public, and his laid-back demeanor only strengthened that bond. His soft voice and nervous energy cre-ated an endearing figure. And he was constantly working. He never stopped. Day, night, he was constantly on, continually plugged in. FTX was headquartered in the beautiful Bahamas, but SBF's skin was cloud-white. It might as well have been in Alaska. He looked pasty at times, hung over not from alcohol but from too many long hours spent staring at screens. His relentless work ethic was just another part of his growing legend, appealing to the hustle culture that crypto enthusiasts embrace. Despite everything, I still respect his immense intellect. He remains one of the most intelligent people I've ever met and, unfortunately, the most troubled, too.

In March 2019, SBF had pitched to Samani and his partners the idea of investing in his startup exchange. It's going to change the world, he told them, and revolutionize the way crypto was bought and sold. But Multicoins declined. They had bet big on another exchange, Binance, the Chinese crypto behemoth, and they were convinced it would be the winner in the exchange space, the coin equivalent of the New York Stock Exchange. In their view, there was no way FTX could effectively compete against it. However, they were deeply impressed by SBF's intelligence and grasp of the cryptocurrency markets. They kept a close eye on FTX as it began to capture market share and increase volumes. Samani started to notice a clear pattern: FTX wasn't just competing; it was winning. Samani had a sinking thought. Did they make a mistake not investing in FTX? Samani wondered if they had backed the wrong horse in Binance. There was one way to find out. If FTX was going to be a credible threat, now was the time to get in. Multicoins bought the FTT token, and Samani set up his Twitter account to receive a daily summary of SBF's tweets, which he would eagerly read every night at 5 p.m.

He noticed that SBF started tweeting a lot about DeFi, often discussing the same nuanced topics that Samani had obsessed over. After declining SBF's offer to lead a seed round, Samani had occasionally reached out to SBF, but the two never connected. After seeing tweets about DeFi applications and concepts, Samani decided to give it another try.

He sent him a direct message on Twitter in May 2020.

"Hey, man. I see you're playing around with DeFi. Glad you're interested. You should check out Solana."

No response from SBF.

Five weeks later, out of the blue, Samani received a DM.

"What was that thing you were talking about. . .Solana?' We're exploring all the other L1s."

Samani immediately set up the call for July 7 between SBF and Yakovenko. When the call began, Yakovenko wasted no time: "I want to build an on-chain Nasdaq. I want to have on-chain limit orders."

"Yes!" SBF immediately responded. "I want to build that, too."

Of course, there were technical issues, most specifically ones related to latency. Every global exchange, whether it trades stocks, bonds, commodities, or currencies, is in a death race against time. Exchanges don't compete over seconds or even fractions of a second. They compete for nanoseconds, or one billionth of a second. For perspective, if you traveled at the speed of light, you would reach Jupiter in just over 40 minutes. That's a long distance in a short amount of time. If you traveled the speed of light for a nanosecond, you would move only a foot. That's how quick it is.

On the call, Samani pushed SBF on this point.

"The problem is Solana's block times are 400 milliseconds," Samani said. "The New York Stock Exchange and Nasdaq compete over nanoseconds. Sam, you run an exchange. You understand the importance of latency for price discovery better than anyone. Can an exchange operator have an on-chain order book when you have 400 milliseconds of latency instead of one millisecond or less?"

SBF froze, his eyes darting skyward, as if observing high-frequency trades zipping through a blockchain. For two agonizing seconds, there was nothing but silence. Finally, his mouth opened, but he didn't say anything. Another two seconds passed. Then, he unleashed a somewhat poetic soliloquy on the wild, untamed nature of high-frequency trading. In that moment, you could almost see the numbers swirling in his head.

"You know," SBF said softly and slowly. "In asset prices, there is a lot of noise. Many trades occur at a sub-400 millisecond time-scale. But a lot of that is just noise. Some of it is fundamental. But a lot of it is just traders moving around."

Another long pregnant pause.

"What matters most, though. . .," another long pause as SBF continued to visualize the technical machinations of an order. "What really matters and the better question is, 'Can you capture information and asset prices onto the blockchain at the rate at which the machines can parse and act on it?' If possible, that would be fine for asset price discovery. The only downside is the market markets won't quote as tight, and the bid-ask spreads might be wider."

In simple terms, what SBF said was "don't lose sight of the forest through the trees." Sure, millions of trades happen in a second, but a lot of them are just noise, one computer jockeying with another for a small amount. The more meaningful trades were the larger blocks that could anchor a position. Market makers would have to account for this by widening the prices at which they bought and sold securities, or what's commonly known as the "bid-ask spread."

Samani and Yakovenko had heard enough. They had found their man.

Yakovenko concluded the call by demonstrating how fast and secure the Solana blockchain was. He used a website called break.solona.com. It was a really simple demo. Every time you tapped a key on the keyboard, a transaction was sent to the block-chain to show you how fast that transaction got confirmed. The system was high-speed and accurate.

SBF interrupted and ended the demonstration.

"We're good," SBF said, indicating he had to attend another meeting. He ended the call by saying aloud, "We're gonna build an on-chain order book on Solana."

Giddy with excitement from the call that stretched to 1 a.m., Samani and Yakovenko went to bed convinced they had found the right partner to take the still-fledgling Solana network to the next level. The events of the next morning only further convinced them.

The following day, Yakovenko pinged Samani.

"Dude. Holy shit!" Yakovenko said.

"What?" Samani replied.

In the short period after the call, FTX's army of engineers attempted to break the Solana blockchain but were unsuccessful.

"This guy moves fast," said Samani.

In August 2020, Multicoin Capital made another sizable investment that would reshape the DeFi landscape. They invested heavily in Serum, a decentralized cryptocurrency exchange built on the Solana blockchain and designed by FTX engineers. The project represented the crypto world's most direct attempt to upend traditional finance by eliminating intermediaries and empowering users to trade, lend, and invest directly on the blockchain. It wasn't the first, but it was the best. Developers had attempted to create trading platforms on the Ethereum network, but the high transaction fees and sluggish processing speeds frustrated both traders and developers. Samani and his partners saw an opportunity to challenge the status quo, and Serum, with its promise of speed, efficiency, and scalability, became their weapon of choice. This would be the trading platform of the future, free of sluggish congestion. It was the world Samani envisioned when he bought Ethereum. It's what drew him to crypto in the first place. It was the promised land.

Serum wasn't just another decentralized exchange. It was also the most direct salvo at Ethereum's grip on DeFi and its constant years of fumbling. Sure, it was faster and more technically advanced than anything that had come before. However, Serum's ambitious scope also acted as a giant magnifying glass, bringing into sharp focus all of Ethereum's shortcomings. Samani couldn't contain his glee, and it wasn't just about the money he was about to make. Serum was the first real example of the promise of the Solana network, live in action, right there for the world to see. It brought the precision and sophistication of traditional financial exchanges to the decentralized world. Multicoin's investment in Serum was a bet on this vision, and it was paying off spectacularly.

From the moment Serum launched, it was clear it was something special. It debuted on August 31, 2020, and on its first day, its native token, SRM, skyrocketed, surging nearly 2,000% and peaking just shy of $4. The market's enthusiasm was palpable. Traders, developers, and investors flocked to the platform. The decentralized future of trading that many had imagined and hoped for was finally here: fast, cheap, and accurate on-chain trading. It was the dream. By 2022, Serum had processed more than $32 billion in trading volume, according to CoinDesk, solidifying its position as the foundation of Solana's rapidly growing DeFi ecosystem. But it wasn't just the numbers that made Serum a game-changer; it was the way it fundamentally redefined what a decentralized exchange could be.

At the heart of Serum's innovation was its Central Limit Order Book, the same feature that has been a mainstay on traditional exchanges, such as the New York Stock Exchange or Nasdaq. It was precisely what Samani and Yakovenko had envisioned when they first met in San Francisco years earlier, and it surpassed anything Ethereum had to offer. Trading on Serum was like driving an F1 race car. Ethereum's DeFi trading platforms? That was like driving a Porsche in rush hour. There was no comparison. The Central Limit Order Book allowed users to place limit orders with precise control over price and quantity. This was a revelation in DeFi, where such granularity had been largely absent. Traders could now execute complex strategies, such as limit and market orders, with the same confidence and precision as they would on a centralized, traditional exchange like the New York Stock Exchange. In essence, Serum had virtualized the rules that had governed trading on conventional exchanges for nearly a century, creating the decentralized Nasdaq that Yakovenko had long dreamed about.

The implications of this design were profound. For nearly a century, centralized exchanges like the Nasdaq, CME, or the New York Stock Exchange have relied on order books to match buyers and sellers. But this was a closed circuit, centralized party, controlled by a handful of institutions and the people who worked for them. Unless you had a seat on the exchange or were a market maker, you were an outsider. Serum's on-chain Central Limit Order Book broke the doors open, offering a decentralized alternative to centralized trading. Now, for the first time on a blockchain, traders can see the full depth of the order book, analyze market trends, and execute trades with minimal slippage, just like their TradFi counterparts. This level of sophistication empowered a new class of DeFi traders, ranging from retail investors to institutions, who could now engage with the market in sophisticated ways previously reserved for Wall Street. Suddenly, trading on the blockchain was no longer a junior varsity affair; Serum provided the same playing field the Wall Street guys had. This drew a new level of investor talent to the platform. Professional and advanced retail traders could feel a real sense of comfort.

The name Serum was also a masterstroke of branding, evoking the image of a concentrated, potent solution—a medical Serum—that could rapidly cure a sick patient. In this case, the patient was the sorry state of affairs of DeFi on the Ethereum platform. Serum injected speed, efficiency, and liquidity into a space that had been swollen shut by Ethereum's high fees and slow speed. Some speculated that the name Serum was intentional, a not-so-subtle jab at Ethereum's struggles. If Ethereum's DeFi ecosystem was a patient suffering from high fees and slow transactions, Serum was the cure, administered with surgical precision by FTX and Solana. In short, Serum was the antidote to all Ethereum's many problems. Whether intentional or not, the metaphor resonated. Where Ethereum users might pay exorbitant gas fees for a single trade, Serum's transactions were lightning-fast and cost pennies, opening the door to a broader range of participants. Small-scale traders, who had been priced out of Ethereum's DeFi ecosystem, could now participate. The platform's low fees and high speeds even allowed for a decentralized version of high-frequency trading and algorithmic strategies that had previously only been executed through traditional exchanges. It was as if the conventional trading system, one that had existed for 100 years, had been virtualized for the modern era.

But Serum's advantages didn't stop at trading. It also tackled one of DeFi's most persistent challenges: interoperability. The platform was designed to enable users to swap assets across different blockchains seamlessly. This meant traders could move tokens native to Solana, Ethereum, and other networks without relying on cumbersome bridges or intermediaries. It was the equity equivalent of allowing purchases of Nasdaq-listed stocks on the New York Stock Exchange. This fluidity was a critical step toward realizing DeFi's full potential, which the technical limitations of individual blockchains had long constrained. By enabling cross-chain asset swaps, Serum positioned itself as a central hub in the increasingly interconnected DeFi landscape. It was the place to be!

Serum's impact exploded through Solana's ecosystem, and soon, a sort of virtuous cycle in the virtual world began. More developed markets gave rise to a greater number of apps, which provided investors with the tools to trade more frequently, a trend that was increasingly occurring. An ecosystem was growing. Solana wasn't just challenging Ethereum; it was crushing it at its own game. For Samani and his partners at Multicoin Capital, this was vindication of their thesis that Solana could challenge Ethereum's dominance as the platform of choice for DeFi and programmable money. Of course, there were setbacks. Ethereum lovers were quick to point out Solana's occasional network outages and vulnerabilities, but those cries felt like sour grapes. Still, Serum's impact on DeFi trading was undeniable. It set a new standard for what a decentralized exchange could achieve, proving that DeFi could rival the speed and sophistication of centralized systems without sacrificing the principles of decentralization.

Multicoins bold bet paid off, but it was more than just a win. It was validation of their investment thesis, not so much about Solana, though they were right about that, too. Instead, it validated their vision of a future where centralized and decentralized trading could coexist, with virtual exchanges functioning alongside physical ones. The future was materializing right before their eyes. The possibilities seemed limitless.

Chapter 5

The Summer of Solana—Go Ape!

Anatoly Yakovenko wasn't supposed to be the guy steering a blockchain through a financial apocalypse. He was a coder, a tinkerer, a guy who liked to build things that worked fast and didn't break. But there he was, in March 2020, sitting in a sparsely furnished office in San Francisco, staring at a computer screen while the world outside collapsed. COVID had already turned the city into a ghost town, and now, just two days after Yakovenko and Gokal launched Solana, the markets decided to stage their version of Armageddon. Bitcoin cratered. Stocks tanked. The world was in the midst of an unprecedented global upheaval. It wasn't just the markets that were crashing; society seemed to be on the verge of collapse. People were dying. Hospitals were clogged. Schools shut down. Amid the chaos, Yakovenko's phone would not stop buzzing with calls from panicked investors. "We don't even know if our fund is going to survive," one of them told him, a voice flat with resignation. No advice. No lifeline. Just the stark reality that Solana, barely born, might already be dead, a victim of much greater forces.

Yakovenko leaned back in his chair, his mind racing. Solana had nine months of cash to keep the lights on, the servers humming, and the team paid. Nine months wasn't much, not when you're trying to build the blockchain of the future. He and Gokal had poured everything into getting to this point. Delaying the launch, waiting for the storm to pass, wasn't an option. It wasn't just the money. It was the momentum, the sheer will it took to drag this thing into existence. "I don't think Raj and I had it in us to just do it again later," Yakovenko would later say, years after the fact, his voice still carrying the weight of someone who'd stared down the abyss.

He had a theory, though, one that sounded crazy amid the chaos but made complete sense to him. The worst time to launch a company is just before a crash. After a crash? Well, that's not so bad. Starting at the bottom, when the world is crumbling, forces you to build lean, be scrappy, and be relentless. It forces you to choose what is essential and what isn't. In raging bull markets, excess creeps in. The money flows, budgets bloat, and you start to think you're better than you are. But at the bottom? Well, every decision can be a matter of life or death. You're not just building a product; you're fighting for survival. It forces you to be smarter, leaner, and more desperate. Yakovenko saw the COVID-19 crash in March 2020 not as a death sentence but as a quiet opportunity. Better to start on the bottom and claw your way up than crash from the top and never recover.

The crypto market was battered, to be sure, but that meant fewer speculators and more committed investors. Launching in a downturn meant they'd have to execute flawlessly. Investors weren't throwing money at crypto in the depths of the 2020 market crash. Every dollar Solana raised came from convincing skeptics, not hype-chasers. That forced clarity from an already lean and dedicated group. Solana's implicit promise to users was to outlast, out scale, and outrun other blockchains; what better time to prove its mettle than amid a global meltdown? Yakovenko was reminded of the old Buffett adage: be fearful when others are greedy and greedy when others are fearful.

And he was reminded of the worst advice that he thankfully never took. Decades earlier, in the midst of the dot-com meltdown, Yakovenko's university professor had passed along some odd advice. In the midst of the stock market meltdown, his professor pulled him aside and suggested to him that maybe tech wasn't the best future to pursue after school. The advice surprised Yakovenko. It seemed so short-sighted from a person who should know better. Everyone can get rich in a bull market. Had he followed that advice, not only would he have walked away from a fortune, but he would've turned his back on the only calling that ever animated every fiber in his body. Tech was his life, and surely it would recover from a crash. Booms and busts are part of the business cycle, whether you're in tech or anything else. Solana may not make it, he thought, but a global market crash would not be the culprit. Heck, he thought, nowhere to go but up!

So, on March 16, 2020, when the stock markets around the world were nearing a multiyear low, Solana went live. It was a quiet debut, overshadowed by the chaos of the pandemic and a crypto market still licking its wounds from the 2018 crash. The native token, SOL, started trading at a modest $0.78. Yakovenko's team was working around the clock, chasing what they called "fire-driven development." The network was processing more than 1,000 transactions per second, still way faster than Ethereum, but problems were ever present. It was like a car with loose lug nuts. Tighten one too much, and the others wouldn't hold. The moment they fixed one problem, another would just as quickly arrive. It was the crypto version of whack-a-mole.

For the first year, Solana was a niche player in the crypto world, a blockchain for those who could swim in the deep end of the pool. Developers tinkered, early adopters staked SOL to bolster the network, and Yakovenko's team worked to iron out kinks. The crypto market was warming up, though, and by early 2021, it was in a veritable bull market. It started with a spark: the NFT craze. Nonfungible tokens (NFTs), digital collectibles like CryptoPunks and Bored Apes, were exploding, mostly on Ethereum.

But Ethereum's gas fees were astronomical, sometimes hundreds of dollars for a single transaction. Solana, with its dirt-cheap fees and blazing speed, looked like a lifeboat. Launching a blockchain is like opening a restaurant in a city already crowded with Michelin-starred establishments. You need more than a good menu; you need buzz, customers, and a bit of luck.

You need an Ape!

Certain years spark instant memories for traders: 1999, the dot-com bubble. In 2001, the dot-com crash. In 2008, the great financial crisis. 2021 is right up there. It was wild, electric even, a captivating mix of audacity, insanity, ambition, innovation, and instant riches. It was a classic boom. It was the Summer of Solana, and it was glorious.

At the center of it all was the Solana network, which was making it all possible. The blockchain was leaving its layer 1 rivals in the dust. In a chaotic bull market marked by surging values for NFTs, SPACs, and Meme stocks, Solana's super-fast network was an island of calm, processing millions of transactions with the precision of a well-tuned Ferrari. And fueling it was a series of Apes. That August, the Degenerate Ape Academy launched on Solana's NFT marketplace. This was more than a moment; it was a cultural earthquake, a phenomenon that would come to define the very fabric of the crypto world. The Degenerate Ape Academy was a riotous collection of cartoon Apes, each bursting with its own outrageously bold swagger.

Some had gold chains, while others wore pirate hats or had laser eyes. They weren't the sleek, status-driven Bored Apes found on Ethereum's marketplace. These Apes were raw, born from the gritty, audacious spirit of Solana's community. These Apes were the digital equivalent of a Basquiat or Warhol, equal parts audacity and absurdity. And the Solana community couldn't get enough. They were lottery tickets masquerading as digital gold, and they were minting millionaires by the minute. It was a mashup of Cabbage Patch dolls, jewelry, and modern art, all combined into one virtual love child. When the mint launched on August 7, it was as if someone had tossed a spark into a fireworks factory. The entire collection sold out in minutes. Millions poured in as speculators feasted on the next big trade. The SOL token, which was valued at just $30 a week earlier, more than doubled to $75 in less than a month. Suddenly, there was a real alternative to clunky Ethereum. Apes squared off in auctions that felt more like heavyweight prize fights than a trading session. Some NFTs would increase 10–20 times their mint price in hours. Social media threads became the new ticker, but instead of stock symbols, users were bombarded with a constant stream of diamond-hand and rocket emojis, pictures of moons, and let's fucking go or "LFG" chants. It was a digital gold rush, live, 24 hours a day on every trader's phone, a messy speculative parade tucked neatly into your pocket. The Apes weren't just pixels or some digital collectible; they were symbols of possibility, proof that Solana's low-cost, super-fast network could democratize wealth creation in ways Ethereum's could never.

Solana's low fees and speed turned it into a playground for anyone with a wallet and an iota of ambition. The Apes weren't just a hit; they were a supernova, and the clearest signal yet that Solana could handle the kind of high-octane, high-hype traffic that would clog up other blockchains. It wasn't the first time a speculative boom had hit a layer 1 (L1) network. Just three years prior, Ethereum had given a hint of what was to come with its 2017 initial coin offering (ICO) boom. Most were worthless tokens, and the short-lived boomlet was better remembered for poking the SEC into action than it was for creating wealth. But if the 2017 ICO boom shined a light on Ethereum's promise, it also highlighted its shortcomings. The network buckled under the weight of its exorbitant gas fees. Transactions clogged up like the Lincoln Tunnel traffic at rush hour. Solana was different. It was designed and engineered for raw speed, capable of processing thousands of transactions per second, with fees so low that they were practically negligible. It was meant for this moment. The Ape mint was a bold declaration to the skeptics who'd dismissed Solana as a pipe dream.

Yakovenko didn't pound his chest. That wasn't his style. But he also didn't need to. The army of Solana Apes was doing that for him.

Everyone took notice. Solana's innovation acted as a magnet for developers, who flocked to the network, all drawn by the promise of a blockchain that could keep pace with their wildest ideas. Retail traders, flush with COVID stimulus checks and fueled by a roaring stock market, dove headfirst into the speculative pool. Journalists, sensing the next big story, wrote daily about this lightning-fast network with a sunny name. Soon, Solana quotes were being displayed on the CNBC ticker, alongside valuable real estate, and more established investments like gold, bonds, and Bitcoin. Solana's moment arrived. New tokens sprouted like wildfire. Different lending protocols popped up every day.

By September, Solana's total market cap topped $63 billion. By November, it hit $74 billion, nearly the same as Uber's, a figure that would've sounded like a joke a year earlier. The SOL token, hovering around $1.50 at the beginning of the year, skyrocketed to $200, a 12,000% surge that seemed like money from heaven for the crypto faithful. Solana elbowed aside Cardano and Dogecoin to claim the title of the fourth-largest cryptocurrency. It was more valuable than General Motors. But the numbers told only half the story. This was a vibe, a futuristic dream expressed through pixelated Apes and the promise of a new financial frontier. Solana was finally being hailed as the Ethereum killer, a title Yakovenko downplayed with a sly grin but never entirely rejected either. The market, ravenous for the next big thing, didn't care about nuance. Solana was scorching hot. Ethereum was not. The hype was a drug, and everyone was hooked. The Degenerate Ape Academy morphed into a status symbol, a badge for those who'd caught the early wave. Top-tier Apes fetched millions at auction. Even established auction houses like Sotheby's, more often associated with priceless Picassos, jumped into the deep end of the NFT pool. The party was open to anyone with a few SOL; anyone could join the frenzy.

For Yakovenko, the Apes were more than a Meme or a byproduct of a market mania. They were irrefutable proof that Solana could simultaneously juggle both the feral energy of Wall Street's trading pits and Main Street's retail armies without breaking a sweat. This was the blockchain he'd envisioned. This was better than on-chain Nasdaq. This was the marketplace of the future, inhabited not by the old guard, who pushed and shoved their way to win a quarter or eighth of a point, but instead by coders and nimble traders, unburdened by tradition and armed with iPhones. Yakovenko thought back to the long nights coding on too many cups of coffee. They had battled the bugs, the naysayers, the litany of technical challenges and sheer exhaustion. They endured ridicule, both in the form of unreturned calls by venture capitalists and open insults on Twitter. Both hurt the same. But he had finally built the playground of the future, and the kids were loving it.

The Ape mint was Solana's baptism by fire. Solana didn't just survive; it thrived. Despite furious volume, fees barely bugged, confirmations were instantaneous, and the network hummed along. For Yakovenko, it was vindication. The Apes proved Solana could handle anything. But Yakovenko's dream stretched beyond NFTs and Meme coins. He envisioned a world where Solana-powered global finance, where established fintech giants like PayPal would have to take notice. The Apes were a stress test, a wild experiment that showed Solana could scale without choking. But beneath the incandescent glow, cracks were forming. Solana's speed was a marvel, but it came at a cost: fragility. Its architecture was like a Formula 1 car, blindingly fast but equally as delicate and prone to catastrophic failure if it hit a pothole.

On September 14, 2021, that pothole arrived. A surge of transactions, reportedly from bots hammering a new token launch, overwhelmed the network. Nodes began to choke, like a streaming service buffering during a live sporting event. By mid-morning, the unthinkable happened. Solana went dark. For 17 agonizing hours, the blockchain hailed as crypto's future was a ghost town. No transactions, no trades, no NFTs, just a deafening silence punctuated by angry tweets and a plummeting SOL price. Ethereum loyalists crowed, their network's plodding reliability suddenly looking like a virtue. On social platforms, Solana became a punchline, memed as the thrilling but unstable upstart, exciting but unreliable, a risky bet for your financial health. The outage was a gut punch, a public humiliation for a project that had soared so high. Ethereum suddenly looked like the old steady girlfriend, safe and secure. Solana seemed more like a supermodel with a drug problem, exciting but exceedingly flaky.

Bleary-eyed in a haze of code and cold coffee, Yakovenko and his team scrambled through the night and raced to restart the network. SOL coins were in free fall, and the broader crypto market offered no cushion. Critics pounced, questioning whether Solana could deliver on its promise of scale without sacrificing stability. The euphoria of the summer suddenly felt like a cautionary tale and a pointed reminder that if something is too good to be true, it likely is. But Yakovenko, ever the stoic engineer, refused to panic. He did what he always did when confronted by a challenge. He worked the problem. Outages were the price of pushing the network to its edge, he told his team. Failure was data, and data was progress, and progress was an open invitation to improve and get better. It was a learning opportunity. Yakovenko didn't sugarcoat it. He didn't make excuses. He worked the problem, deploying fixes and running various tests. Trust is crypto's lifeblood, and the Solana outage was undermining it. Yet, for Yakovenko, the outages weren't death sentences; they were lessons.

The road to his vision, a blockchain that could serve as both Wall Street's and Main Street's marketplace, was littered with potholes and pitfalls, but Yakovenko viewed them more as opportunities than problems. The summer had shown what was possible, with the Degenerate Ape Academy igniting a torrent of trading activity. Still, it also highlighted just how much more work remained to be done. The Solana faithful, including my firm and I, never lost faith. Was it at times humbling and maybe even a little embarrassing? Sure. However, I was reminded of Bitcoin's many struggles in the past, with the occasional exchange hack spiking investor concerns and eroding its narrative as a secure global store of value. Solana's crash had a similar effect. It undermined its narrative as a superhighway for trade. The Solana team's reputation was on the line, and the crypto world was watching.

By September 15, Solana flickered back to life, but the scars lingered. The cryptocurrency world watched skeptically, wondering if Solana could claw its way back from the depths of the abyss. The army of Apes shined a light on Solana's shortcomings, but rather than run from them, Yakovenko and team embraced them and used the whole setback as an opportunity to get even better. The network got stronger and better. The bots may have temporarily broken the network, but they also made it stronger. Amid the turmoil was a clear takeaway: chaos breeds progress. And Solana was here to stay.

The whole ordeal also underscored something equally important: management's resolve. Yakovenko and his team never panicked. They didn't point fingers or cry foul at the bots. They played the hand they were dealt and won. They did what they always did; they worked harder. Ethereum lovers could hardly contain their glee on Twitter. Critics howled. It was a humbling moment for sure, but Yakovenko saw it as a puzzle to solve, not a defeat in which to wallow. "Every crash is a teacher," he told his team.

The outage wasn't a one-off. In 2022, Solana would face nine more outages, including a seven-hour blackout in May caused by bots and a four-hour crash in June. Each failure chipped away at Solana's aura, feeding a narrative that it was fast but flaky, a sprinter who kept tripping over its shoelaces. To Yakovenko, each stung like a large paper cut. But if speed was the network's superpower, resilience was a close second. It was like a Timex. It took its licking and kept on ticking. It could take a punch. It was fast and durable. And it would only grow stronger.

My partners and I approached the opportunity in the same way we did when facing the many setbacks in Bitcoin: we bought the dip furiously. I was reminded of the words of the great George

Soros (you may hate him or love him, many do, but he is one of the all-time great investors) and his timeless advice to any investor: "If an asset should die and it doesn't, it should be bought." It was a refrain often used among Bitcoin investors, and the point was simple. If something can rebound from a crash multiple times, get punched in the face, and get right back up, it's likely a mispriced and misunderstood asset. And that resilience imparts an intrinsic value to the asset class itself. Consider the numerous times Amazon crashed in the late 1990s and early 2000s. But it came back. Because it wasn't just a stock, and Amazon wasn't just an online store. It was a glimpse of the future, innovation personified. The future is messy and uncertain, two things investors hate. But the companies that survive emerge the strongest. Amazon became one of the most transformative forces in all of commerce. It disrupted and redefined countless industries, all from a company founded in a garage that initially just sold physical books (remember those?). Innovation will never stop, and when paired with passion and brilliant management, you have the makings of a generationally successful trade. And Solana's right there.

The Summer of Solana could've been the end for the network. Turns out, it was just the beginning. But the most significant setback of all was yet to come. It would be the most devastating strike yet, and it came from the hand of Solana's most prominent backer and one of my closest business partners.

Chapter 6

The Tweet Heard Around the World

Istared at my phone, a mix of horror and disbelief on my face. "You hearing this about FTX?"

Then another text.

"What's Sam doing?"

FTX was in trouble. Liquidity issues. A possible run on deposits. My phone started buzzing with more texts from friends in the industry and journalists. I didn't have answers, but I had a stake in the outcome. Sam Bankman-Fried (SBF) owned a chunk of my business. Equally important, he owned a part of my reputation, and both were at risk. I liked and trusted him. I opened my Rolodex for him. I thought I knew him well; he had lovely and loving parents. He was odd, a glance revealed that, but his quirkiness conveyed a soft gentleness and honesty. After all, if he couldn't conceal his twitches, how could he conceal a crime? SBF preached effective altruism and gave away millions to charitable causes. He was either genuine or a genuine sociopath.

So, when CoinDesk, the leading crypto industry publication, published an article on November 2, 2022, revealing that FTX and its sister company, Alameda Research, were co-mingling customer deposits, at first I didn't believe it, or, more accurately, I didn't want to believe it. But others did, and the headline reverberated like a nuclear explosion, destroying confidence in the relatively unregulated and opaque crypto markets. Fears grew. A bank run, a concept that had crippled financial institutions for centuries, found a modern and unfamiliar target: crypto. FTX customers began to pull money. And what started as a fire quickly turned into an inferno when Changpeng "CZ" Zhao, the CEO of rival exchange Binance, took to Twitter and blowtorched what remained of FTX.

"Due to recent revelations that have come to light, we have decided to liquidate any remaining FTT on our book," CZ tweeted four days later, referring to FTX's native token.

The dagger wasn't just shoved into the heart; it was twisted.

I couldn't sit around and wait. I made the unilateral decision to fly down to the Bahamas, where FTX was headquartered. It was a rescue situation, and I maybe could help. SkyBridge had no assets custodied at FTX, thank God. I'd seen enough conflicts of interest in my Wall Street days to avoid that trap, but SkyBridge still had significant exposure, and I needed to know firsthand what was happening.

I landed in Nassau on Tuesday morning, the air thick with heat and humidity. I could feel the dread in my stomach. When I arrived at FTX's headquarters, it was a circus, a scene out of my worst nightmare. Staffers were darting around, laptops left open, phones ringing off the hook. I had expected some measure of chaos, but this was something else. There were two camps: SBF's inner circle, tight-lipped and pale, and everyone else, who looked like they'd just seen a ghost. I caught up with some of the legal and compliance folks, people I had met through my many dealings with SBF. Their faces told me more than their words. "It's not just a liquidity issue," one of them muttered, eyes darting. "There's. . .stuff we didn't know." *Stuff* is never a good word in finance.

I saw SBF briefly. He was a wreck, hair wilder than usual, his pitch-black eyes wide open and bloodshot, pacing aimlessly around the office. He looked like he had just emerged from a war zone, completely shell-shocked, and I briefly recalled the opening scene in *Saving Private Ryan*. I didn't know what I was looking at. I didn't confront him. That's not my style, especially when a guy's already down, but I did talk to him.

"What's going on, Sam?" I asked.

"Miscalculations," he mumbled, and then proceeded to spew out a torrent of technical terms that was followed by some nonsensical speech about how he and the team were going to "fix it."

"Fix what, Sam? What happened?"

More mumbling. He was talking so quickly, and none of it made sense. He was contrite, but he didn't seem to grasp the gravity of what was happening. It was as if he was trying to escape a burning building by solving a complex math problem. Later, he addressed the firm over Zoom, a firm-wide speech that sounded more like a plea than a plan. I listened, but my gut was churning.

By midday, the picture was clearer, and it was a grim one. I didn't stick around. I booked a flight back to New York that afternoon, my head spinning. On the plane, I stared out the window, replaying every interaction with SBF, wondering what I missed, what I should've noticed. Looking back, there were what in hindsight could be called red flags: No CFO? No board? SBF's team had brushed that off. They didn't believe in TradFi titles. They were about work, not fancy titles. Crazy, looking back, but it seemed almost admirable at the time. They were young people. They didn't need titles, blah blah. If you wanted titles, there were hundreds of banks with millions of vice presidents. FTX's list of investors was a who's who of moneyed Wall Street: Softbank, BlackRock, Carlyle. We'd all drunk the Kool-Aid, seduced by the promise of a new financial order and a wunderkind who turned out to be more a phony than a prophet. Crypto was having its worst week ever, and I was left wondering if we'd ever recover.

And then things got even stranger.

An X notification popped up on my phone. A retweet. Then another followed, followed by a nonstop avalanche of texts from friends and investors. My phone wouldn't stop vibrating, a constant tremor signaling an oncoming earthquake. I picked it up and stared at the screen in disbelief. It was a series of posts from SBF that seemed half-confession, half-provocation.

I'm sorry. That's the biggest thing.
I fucked up, and I should have done better.

My eyes froze. I couldn't believe what I was looking at. Another pulse indicating an incoming text. I toggled back to iChat. Fifty unread messages. The post was being reposted and commented on 1,000 times a second. It almost seemed alive—F-bombs and death threats. Question marks and sad emojis flooded my feed. He immediately started trending.

Then, just as soon as the first SBF post arrived, before I could begin to process it, another popped up.

I also should have been communicating more very recently.
Transparently — my hands were tied during the duration of the possible Binance deal; I wasn't particularly allowed to say much publicly. But of course it's on me that we ended up there in the first place.

Huh? Another round of reposts and comments, all as incredulous as the first. The torrent of invective almost seemed to leap off my phone. And before I could even begin to process that one, another post! And another. A series of them proceeded to explain what happened.

The full story here is one I'm still fleshing out every detail of, but on a high level, I fucked up twice?

Fucked up twice? What did that mean? Did he admit to fucking up the first time? I couldn't stop staring at the post. It was like reading an ancient text, each passage revealing some new and deeper meaning. Was this a confession? Was he on drugs? Did his lawyers approve this? Was his account hacked? None of it made any sense. I was in a daze, confused and angry at the same time. Back home, I started piecing it together. The X posts, the news reports, and the industry chatter all pointed to a disaster that might have started months earlier, possibly as far back as April or May, when another crypto hedge fund, Three Arrows Capital, went bankrupt. At the time, I didn't know if it was fraud, a very specific legal term, but I knew it was betrayal, and not just of me; it was a betrayal of the entire industry.

I spent the next few days doing damage control. My legal team was working to buy back SBF's stake, to unwind the deal, and to get him off our cap table. I went on CNBC, told the world I was distressed, and urged SBF and his family, his parents, Joe and Barbara, good people, to come clean. "Get in front of a regulator," I said. "Tell the truth. Stop the tweets." If SBF believed in effective altruism, like he'd preached, he'd own this mess.

The collapse of FTX was a body blow, but it wasn't the first time I've felt the brute force of a gut punch. I'd survived Wall Street setbacks, an embarrassingly short stint in the White House, and countless career near-death moments. This was different, for sure. This implosion felt personal, a betrayal not only of my trust in SBF but also in the future I so fervently believed in. I could hear the haters. "It's a scam!" "Fake Money!" But I never wavered. SkyBridge doubled down on its crypto strategy, but with a sharper eye for due diligence. I owned my mistake, but my faith in the space was never broken. In fact, it was rewarded. The FTX fallout exposed crypto's regulatory blind spots, and I seized the opportunity to reiterate the need for sensible regulation and oversight, testifying before Congress and writing op-eds. This would not shape my firm's future or the industry's future. I live by a simple rule. If you make a mistake, own it. Don't try to downplay it; don't run from it. Lean into it. Learn from it, but never, ever hide it. Within a year, SkyBridge was thriving again, its crypto portfolio leaner but stronger. The scars remained, but the skin is now tougher.

The collapse of FTX didn't just shake my world; it sent shockwaves through the entire crypto community, from passionate investors to cautious regulators. The betrayal cut deep. The crypto faithful, who'd staked their dreams on decentralized ideals, saw their trust vanish overnight. On X, the pain was visceral. Posts cried out about "lost life savings" and "shattered futures," while others implored the faithful to buy and "HODL." Regulators, long skeptical of crypto's Wild West culture, seized the moment to tighten their grip. The FTX fiasco wasn't merely one man's failure; it laid bare the vulnerabilities of a new and untested industry. Yet, from the wreckage, resilience emerged. Investors like me recalibrated. The crypto community, battered but unbroken, united, forging a stronger, smarter path forward.

Fortunately, others in the industry shared the same sentiment.

Kristin Smith was 30,000 feet above the Atlantic, wedged into a narrow airplane seat, her laptop casting a soft glow in the dim cabin. The air was still and calm, and the engine's drone created a tranquil environment that was the perfect contrast to the pandemonium playing out on her laptop screen. As executive director of the Blockchain Association, Smith was constantly glued to her screens, and what she was looking at was a veritable horror show. FTX was collapsing, seemingly overnight. Was it Enron? A complete accounting scam? Or was it Bear Stearns, an overleveraged, poorly run institution that took on too much risk? It was unclear, but whispers of liquidity cracks had erupted into a full-on dam break. Binance had yanked its bailout lifeline, and users were trapped in a digital limbo, unable to withdraw funds. Allegations were also circulating that SBF had siphoned billions in customer deposits to prop up his hedge fund, Alameda Research. Smith, a DC insider, felt a sharp pulse of vindication. She had always suspected something was amiss with SBF. His altruistic posturing rubbed her as insincere at best. She'd share her concerns in private, but they were almost always dismissed. But at 30,000 feet, none of that mattered. She did not feel the thrill of being right, nor did she feel vindication. She felt dread. The FTX collapse wasn't just SBF's downfall; it was a cruise missile heading right at crypto's fragile credibility, and as the industry's chief advocate, Smith knew she'd be sifting through the rubble for years.

Her laptop was a nonstop parade of X posts and Slack messages. The anger had never been more palpable. At any moment, she half expected one of the angry posts would reach out of her screen and demand their money back. Solana was in the crosshairs. Its token price was in a freefall, erasing much of the euphoria from the Summer of Solana. Smith's mind toggled from the past to the present and back again. She thought back to those dark days of the Spring of 2020, when the world was reeling under the COVID pandemic. The markets were crashing, with stocks and crypto plummeting. Death, both literally and financially, seemed like a real possibility. That's when she first heard of Solana, from an intern who wouldn't stop talking about it. She and he were the only two people in the office. Through masks and several feet of distance, they would often talk about new and exciting L1 protocols. He'd repeatedly talk about this new platform that he couldn't stop messing around with, Solana. The kid was barely old enough to buy a beer. "It's a rocket, Kristin," he'd say, his voice brimming with enthusiasm as he pulled up trading charts on a laptop plastered with crypto stickers. "Thousands of transactions a second, fees cheap as can be." Solana had just launched. Smith, her mind stuck instead on headlines of ventilator shortages and economic collapse, was unmoved. What a godawful time to launch, she thought, picturing the despair the Solana team must have felt over the poor timing.

Smith wasn't a crypto zealot. She was a Washington pragmatist, a former Senate staffer who'd swapped Capitol Hill's marble corridors for the wilder frontier of crypto advocacy. The Blockchain Association's office in 2020 was a spartan outpost, a few desks jammed into a corner of DCs lobbying district. The setting was relatively modest, standing in contrast to the organization's bold calls to open up the crypto industry. Smith's mission was to translate the arcane world of tokens and ledgers into legislation that senators, many of whom knew nothing of blockchains, could swallow. In the meantime, her clients were the big industry players, a mix of large and small companies, some with big egos, others more strategic, all united in a common desire to see a bigger crypto industry. She was a tightrope walker, balancing the whims of Silicon Valley with the gatekeepers of Washington. Most days consisted of back-to-back calls and meetings that began well before dawn.

As she saw the torrent of tweets light up her screen, Smith recalled her first encounter with SBF, at Bitcoin 2021 in Miami, a conference that felt like a crypto Burning Man. She was grabbing coffee when she spotted him: cargo shorts, a mop of curly hair, and a carefully disheveled look that was becoming his signature style, as he chatted with another executive. FTX, his exchange, was the talk of the town, a juggernaut eating Binance's lunch. Smith introduced herself, intrigued by his reputation as a prodigy who'd turned arbitrage into billions. Bankman-Fried was polite but distracted, his eyes darting around, seemingly disconnected from his mouth. Later, she invited him to a fundraiser at her apartment, expecting him to be a no-show. To her surprise, he showed up, a minor celebrity in a room of crypto insiders, his awkward charisma pleasing the crowd.

Over the next year, Smith's relationship with SBF soured. As the Blockchain Association's CEO, she was focused on advancing the entire crypto industry, not just one player. But SBF's DC strategy was a one-man blitz, relentlessly FTX-centric, a campaign that prioritized his empire over the ecosystem. His regulatory proposals, she warned colleagues, were poison for decentralized finance and smaller players. SBF didn't take kindly to her pushback, and their conversations grew increasingly tense. By October 2022, when Bankman-Fried breezed into a DC hotel conference room for a policy meeting, Smith's patience had run its course. The room was your typical DC hotel sterile box, all beige carpet and fluorescent lights. He stayed for 45 minutes, talked over everyone, and left without listening, his cargo shorts a defiant middle finger to the room's buttoned-up vibe. He's managing his image, not solving problems, Smith thought, her distrust hardening into a palpable dislike.

Solana, unfortunately, was caught in SBF's orbit. FTX and Alameda were major backers of Solana projects, and SBF's embrace of the blockchain had partly fueled the Summer of Solana's meteoric rise. Smith's early skepticism about Solana, born in that COVID-era office, lingered because of its FTX ties. She saw it as a tool of SBF's empire. That perception held until the FTX collapse, when Solana's resilience forced her to take a fresh look. But back on that November 2022 flight, as the crypto world unraveled, Smith's mind flickered between vindication and dread. She'd been right about SBF, but the fallout was a catastrophe. Crypto's credibility, already fragile in DC, was in tatters. The Blockchain Association's first annual summit was weeks away, and Smith and her colleagues were already rewriting speeches, recalibrating their pitch to a room of skeptical policymakers. The plane's cabin felt like a pressure cooker, the hum of engines a counterpoint to the chaos on her screen. Solana, hammered by its ties to FTX, was a poster child for the carnage, with its token price in a death spiral. Yet, even as the market bled, Smith couldn't ignore Solana's resilience. She remembered the network's 17-hour outage in September 2021. Now, facing a scandal that would've buried lesser blockchains, Solana was showing signs of life.

The Summer of Solana had been a proving ground, a stress test that showed Solana could handle the kind of high-volume traffic that turned Ethereum into a digital quagmire. The Degenerate Ape mint was its defining moment, a cultural explosion that pushed the network to its limits. Solana didn't just survive; it thrived, with its fees staying under a penny and confirmations flashing in milliseconds. That resilience was what drew developers, who saw Solana as a blank canvas for their wildest ideas. By 2025, Smith would marvel at the numbers: two-thirds of all blockchain transactions were happening on Solana, a stat that defied gravity. It wasn't because Solana was a first mover; it wasn't. It was because the network had staggered out of the FTX wreckage, bloodied but unbowed, proving its range and potential. From Meme coins to BlackRock's tokenized money market funds, Solana was a crucible for innovation, a blockchain that could juggle Wall Street's trading frenzy and Main Street's NFTs without breaking a sweat.

Solana didn't die. Against all odds, it clawed its way back. In 2023, the crypto winter thawed, and Solana rode the wave. Its price rose 770%, hitting $101 by year's end. The ecosystem rebounded, with daily active wallets tripling and DeFi activity surging. Traders and investors returned, lured by the playful energy of Meme coins. More established brands moved into the platform. Solana demonstrated one of the most essential qualities for any type of investment, crypto or otherwise: resiliency. What you can't kill only comes back stronger. Solana's struggles turned out to be nothing more than a scar or deep callous. It hardened its surface and galvanized its community.

In some ways, Solana's journey is a microcosm of crypto itself: a heady mix of genius, greatness, and growing pains. Yakovenko's vision of a blockchain of the future is still a work in progress, but the fact that Solana has survived its own worst moments, including outages, scandals, and a market meltdown, says something. In fact, it says a lot.

Chapter 7

Tokenization: The Next Frontier

Wall Street used to be a members-only club, and I don't mean that in terms of socio-economic standing. There have always been plenty of working-class kids who make it big on Wall Street; I'm proof of that. Wall Street is the ultimate meritocracy. It doesn't matter if your last name has too many vowels, as mine does. It doesn't matter if you went to a state school or if you're a man of Harvard, as I'm proud to say I am. The members club I'm talking about has nothing to do with lineage and everything to do with access to information. Wall Street's business model is predicated on opacity. If you are a club member, you get the insider's price. If you're not? Good luck. That was part of why I launched SkyBridge: to give smaller investors the same opportunities as larger ones. I wanted to provide them access to the best investment options at competitive prices. In my small way, I was democratizing the market for the not-so-little guy. Since its inception, Wall Street has really been about only one thing: connecting people who need money with those who have it, for a small fee, of course. Commissions on Wall Street used to be fixed. Then came May Day, when the

Securities and Exchange Commission (SEC) forced exchanges and brokerage houses to replace fixed commissions with negotiated ones. It was a seismic shift that had much of Wall Street kicking and screaming. No more easy money! Now, competition for fees would increase. The innovative firms would lean into technology to find efficiencies that could be passed along to win new business. The dumb ones went out of business or merged. Darwin was coming to Wall Street, and he was taking no prisoners.

However, the change sparked a fiercely competitive period. Relationships weren't enough to win business. You had to beat on price and service. You had to work harder and smarter. The game was opening up. Of course, technology has always made markets more efficient. There's a reason why in the past 20 years, commissions have tumbled from $100 to buy a share of stock to nothing today. Despite the advancements, equity trading is not without friction, but it is better than most markets. As assets become more expensive, they tend to become less liquid, and the commission to buy them increases. Ever try purchasing a corporate bond? How about something even more illiquid, like a piece of art or a home? How about an entire building, or even a private company? How about a Rolex? Buying any of these requires a team of lawyers, brokers, and middlemen, along with a reservoir of patience.

These industries are protected by the fortress of gatekeepers and middlemen who are obsessed with keeping prices high, opacity low, and commissions fat. And that's what's so exciting about crypto: the process of tokenization is changing the game, opening up asset classes and shedding light on the abyss of inefficiency and greed. Tokenization involves converting something valuable, such as real estate, stocks, art, or even a watch, into digital "tokens" on a blockchain. These tokens are akin to shares in a company or a deed to a house, but they exist on the Internet, secured by code, and anyone with a crypto wallet can purchase a piece. It's finance, but faster, cheaper, and open to anyone who knows the way of the coin.

In my opinion, tokenization will do for hard assets what the stock market did for corporations hundreds of years ago: unleash a torrent of capital and unlock the economy's true potential. Once you understand how it works and why Solana is key to its success, you'll know why I'm so excited about this trade. So, let's begin with some basics.

Tokenization may sound complicated and vaguely futuristic, but the concept is quite simple, and there are examples of it in our everyday lives. Stock ownership is a crude and early form of tokenization dating back to the Dutch settlers. Back then, the Dutch East India Company, a trading behemoth, was amassing a fortune by selling spices, silks, and furs from around the world, but it needed cash to fund its global endeavors. So, to raise more capital, the early Dutch traders sold shares or company stock to other wealthy Dutch investors and traders. Now, before stocks, if you wanted to invest in a company, you needed a serious amount of money, particularly if it involved a shipping or trading company. And if the ship sank, you had a serious problem. Stocks flipped that script. The Dutch East India Company issued shares, which represented small pieces of ownership, and sold them to anyone with the necessary funds. If you bought a share, you owned a sliver of the company's profits, ships, and future. Suddenly, regular folks, not just barons, could invest. Selling shares democratized ownership and profits, shared risk, and provided more capital.

The last point is key. By increasing the number of investors, the Dutch East India Company created a financial concept that would forever guide every investment: liquidity. Shares began to trade in unofficial settings, such as bars, taverns, or even under trees. A hundred years later, traders established a formal setting that effectively served as crude versions of what would later become stock exchanges. Trading was informal, conducted in coffeehouses or via handwritten agreements, but it laid the groundwork for later exchanges, such as the New York Stock Exchange, which began in 1792. Early stock trading, though clunky and elite-driven, sparked American capitalism, turning big ideas into ownable assets. It fueled the Industrial Revolution and set a young America on its path to financial greatness.

And little has changed since. Think the iPhone is a fantastic device and want to buy an Apple? You'll need three trillion dollars to buy the whole company. But if you're going to own a piece of it, however, and partake in its profits and growth, you can buy one share of Apple, of which there are 15 billion available to purchase. The one share entitles you to a tiny sliver of Apple's profits and future growth. It even allows you to vote on corporate matters. It confers ownership, however small, and it's recorded on a vast ledger between various broker-dealers. Anyone can buy a slice; all you need is a brokerage account.

Now, instead of an Industrial Revolution, a Virtual Revolution is afoot, and it's happening on the blockchain. Tokenization is the new version of stocks, but it uses far better technology and allows for ownership of illiquid assets and revenue streams. Instead of just companies, anything can be sliced up—a sky-scraper, a vineyard, a Picasso, or even royalties on your next great idea. Using blockchain technology, investors break down assets into digital tokens, like shares but with enhanced features and functionality. Each token is a fraction of the asset, secured by code, and unlike stocks, it's tradable anytime, anywhere, so long as you have an Internet connection: no broker, no bank, just a crypto wallet and a click.

Why is this better? Stocks are great, but they're tied to exchanges with centralized gatekeepers that can increase fees. Tokenization changes all of that. It's global, instant, and cheap, with smart con-tracts handling payouts. No middlemen. Just pure decentralized finance, with profits going straight to your wallet automatically. Of course, there are some trade-offs. Equities might be stodgy, but the legal framework around them is second to none. The laws are clear. The legal framework surrounding tokenization remains somewhat unclear, but I suspect that will become clearer as more crypto legislation takes effect. Still, investors are excited because tokenization is like taking the stock market's best attribute, fractional ownership, and making it universal, all powered by blockchain, which ensures security and transparency.

At its core, tokenization is about turning something valuable, such as a building, a piece of art, or even future earnings from a movie, into fractional, tradable ownership units, which is precisely what digital tokens are. There are two main types of tokens. First, there are fungible tokens, like dollar bills: each one is worth the same as the next. For example, a token tied to a building's rental income is fungible; 10 tokens are just 10 tokens, no matter which ones you hold. Then there are non-fungible tokens, or NFTs, which are unique, like a one-of-a-kind baseball card. An NFT might be a digital artwork or a concert ticket, where each one is special, different, and unique.

Tokenization typically employs fungible tokens to break down large assets into smaller, more affordable pieces. Imagine a $500 million office tower in Chicago. In the past, only millionaires or large investment funds could afford to buy into something like that. Now, through the miracle of tokenization, small investors can buy a sliver of that tower, let's say each worth $100, just like a banker might divide up a company into a large number of shares. A teacher in Ohio, a programmer in India, or a retiree in Florida can buy a few tokens and own a slice of the building. The blockchain keeps track of ownership, and a smart contract handles tasks such as sending out rental payments or confirming ownership. But this isn't just about buildings. You can tokenize other physical objects, such as cars or wine barrels. You can also tokenize virtual assets, such as music royalties or video game items, or even more abstract concepts like carbon credits or patents. It's a way to make once inaccessible investments, either because they were too expensive or because they are difficult to trade, available to anyone with a smartphone and some cryptocurrency.

To see how this works, let's use an example. A vineyard owner in Napa Valley needs $2 million to expand their winery. Instead of begging a bank for a loan or selling part of their business to a venture capitalist, they decide to tokenize. First, they choose an asset; in this case, let's use future sales from their next batch of wine, which they expect will generate $2 million over five years. They can sell tokens that represent a share of that money. Next, they create a smart contract that says, "There are 2 million tokens, each worth $1 of future wine sales. Buy a token, and you'll get a tiny fraction, 0.00005%, of the revenue, paid monthly in USDC." The contract is uploaded to the Solana network or any other blockchain.

The owner would then list their tokens on a cryptocurrency exchange or online marketplace. Investors buy in either through a stable coin, SOL, or some other blockchain's native currency. A wine expert in Paris might spend $1,000 for 1,000 tokens, while a New York investment firm might acquire an even larger share, say, 500,000 tokens. Through tokenization, the vineyard owner can raise $1.8 million, enough to fund the expansion. As the wine sells, the money flows into the smart contract, which automatically splits it among token holders (investors) based on how many tokens they own. The Paris wine expert might earn $10 a month if sales are good, while the investment firm would likely receive a much higher amount, as it owns more tokens. The blockchain records every transaction, so it's all transparent. No one can cheat. Even better, those tokens can be traded in a secondary market, injecting even more liquidity. If the wine expert needs cash, they can sell their tokens at a profit if the winery becomes a hit. The smart contract ensures the new buyer receives the revenue rights, eliminating the need for a lawyer. No middleman. Just pure profits.

This is tokenization in action, and it's popping up everywhere. Real estate companies are tokenizing buildings. Artists are tokenizing artwork, and startups are tokenizing future profits. It's flexible, too. The vineyard owner could offer token holders special perks, such as free winery tours or even a vote on what wine to produce next. It's like a game where you can design the rules, make investing fun, and impart technological creativity to your business.

Smart contracts are the magic behind this. You can think of them as those old vending machines that used to line bars or bowling alleys. You put in money, and it gives you something back, like cigarettes, snacks, or even drinks. Smart contracts replace the physical vending machine. For the vineyard owner, the smart contract handles everything; it distributes tokens when investors make payments, sends revenue to token holders, enforces the rules to prevent cheating, and logs all transactions on the blockchain for everyone to see. It's called "trustless" because you don't have to trust a person, just the code. But here's where it gets tricky. That code has to be perfect. A mistake can let hackers steal money. Once the contract is in effect, it's challenging to modify, and it can't handle unexpected events, such as a fire at the vineyard, unless those scenarios are explicitly programmed into the original contract. Investors love smart contracts because they eliminate the need for expensive middlemen, such as lawyers and transfer agents, make transactions transparent, and expedite the process. But this can be tricky, too; a bad contract is like a vending machine that takes your money and gives you nothing in return.

Still, the prospect of cutting out middlemen and infusing assets and industries with liquidity and cash is making many investors salivate. Assets like real estate or private companies were once difficult to sell, much like trying to offload a yacht. Tokenization turns them into tiny slivers of ownership that you can trade anytime, anywhere. Second, it opens doors. A $100 token can get you a piece of a fancy condo or a famous painting, letting regular people invest in things only the rich could touch before. Third, it saves money. Old-school finance is full of middlemen like banks, brokers, and lawyers, all charging high fees. Smart contracts perform tasks for almost nothing, especially on Solana, where transaction fees are extremely low. Fourth, it's global. A tokenized vineyard in Napa can attract buyers from Brazil, China, or Kenya, creating a huge pool of money. Finally, it's just cool. It's like the iPhone when it first hit the scene.

It mesmerized you with endless possibilities. Tokenization reminds me of the app economy 15 years ago. It's just getting started, and I suspect it will get much bigger as a younger generation of mobile phone-facing investors enter the marketplace.

Of course, there are bumps in the road. Not every tokenized market has a large number of buyers and sellers, so prices can fluctuate significantly. Opening investing to everyone is great, but the less experienced might not understand the technology and could fall prey to scams. The traditional middleman, lawyers and bankers, are gone, but coders and engineers will try to work in their fees when designing certain contracts or platforms, so read the fine print. Some countries ban crypto or limit foreign investments, and the tech is young, so not every idea works out. Still, tokenization will open up new markets for asset owners and investors alike, and the super-fast and cheap Solana network will be the chief beneficiary.

Chapter 8

The Meme King

It was late October 2023, and Joe McCann was staring at a cartoon dog. Not just any dog, mind you, but the logo for BONK, a Meme coin that had exploded onto the Solana blockchain. The logo was ridiculous, almost defiantly so: a bulbous, anime-style Shiba Inu with a giant smirk that drenched in the kind of garish yellow and red you'd find on a McDonald's sign. There was a smiley face, three exclamation points that looked vaguely like a pawprint, and an overall aesthetic that screamed, "I dare you to take me seriously." To most people, it was a digital doodle, the kind of thing you'd swipe past on Reddit while doom scrolling. To Joe McCann, it was like an ancient scripture, a Rosetta Stone of the Internet age, teaming with hidden meaning. Every glance revealed a new layer, the exaggerated curve of the snout, the sly tilt of the head, the way the colors clashed. To the world, it was a cartoon. To McCann, it was money.

Joe McCann wasn't your typical Wall Street guy. He didn't wear pinstripes or spend hours in front of a Bloomberg terminal. He didn't have an MBA from Wharton or a corner office with a view of the Statue of Liberty. Instead, he was a 40-something bald dude who liked to DJ on the weekends and possessed an almost obsessive eye for graphic design. He could riff on Bauhaus architecture one minute and dissect a bid-ask spread the next. He'd grown up in Humboldt County, California, a hippie enclave where tie-dye was like a uniform. The son of a single mom, McCann and his four brothers lived a nomadic childhood, criss-crossing the country and attending 13 schools in seven states by the time he was 18. That kind of instability could crush a kid, make them retreat into themselves, and turn them shy or bitter. Not McCann. It made him a social chameleon, turning him into a human Richter scale capable of measuring cultural currents. He could rate how cool something was. He could walk into a high school in Kansas or a coffee shop in California and instantly clock the cool kids, the ones who set the trends without trying. He could tell you why a pair of sneakers caught fire or why a slang word flopped, and he could do it with a watchmaker's pre-cision. When he looked at BONK's goofy dog, he saw more than a logo. He saw a pattern, a signal in the noise, and it was screaming one thing: buy!

McCann founded Asymmetric Financial, a crypto-focused hedge fund that, in 2023, rode the crypto wave so well that it ditched all competitors in the dust. BONK was the crest of that wave. The Meme coin had quadrupled in value in a matter of weeks, its market cap rocketing from $28 million to $2 billion in the blink of an eye. What did it do? Nothing, as far as anyone could tell. When journalists, with their notepads and furrowed brows, asked McCann that question, he'd snap, "Stupid ques-tion!" as if they'd asked why water was wet. What does it do? It goes higher. A lot higher. That was the whole point of Meme coins. They are cryptocurrencies born from the fevered corners of the Internet, inspired by GIFs, and represent the kind of pop-culture genius that makes you laugh before you pause to wonder if you're part of some grand simulation. They were the digital equivalent of Chia Pets from the '80s or Beanie Babies from the

'90s, except now they came with a blockchain and a market cap. And McCann, with his 20 years of trading experience, his stints at top-tier design agencies, and an almost pathological obsession with Internet culture, was the perfect guy to surf this bizarre new market.

This wasn't his first rodeo. McCann had been around markets long enough to know that value is something that defies logic and doesn't fit neatly into an investor's portfolio. Why does a Picasso fetch $100 million, while a Braque, painted by a guy who was practically in Picasso's shadow, languishes at $10 million? Because it's a Picasso, and people believe the next buyer will pay more. Meme coins were the same. They run on belief, on the collective delirium of crowds who see a dog wearing a hat and think "This is the future!" And McCann had an uncanny knack for spotting the dogs.

Meme coins began with a dog named Kabosu. In 2010, a Japanese kindergarten teacher posted a photo of her Shiba Inu on her blog. The dog was sprawled on a couch, head tilted, eyes narrowed in a squint that seemed to say "What is this nonsense?" or maybe it was "I know something you don't." The Internet went berserk. The photo went viral on Reddit, garnering thousands of likes, shares, and comments. Why? Nobody could pin it down. Maybe it was the dog's expression, which captured some ineffable truth about the human condition. Maybe it was just adorable. But McCann saw something deeper: a simple and lucrative pattern. America loves dogs. Snoopy. Lassie. Even Cujo has a place in our collective hearts. Dogs are woven into the cultural fabric, embedded in our DNA from a 10,000-year partnership that began well before the pyramids, when Earth was still encased in ice. They're loyal. They're relatable. They're a shortcut to the heart. Now, take that primal connection and plug it into the Internet, a technology built to amplify anything to absurdity, and you've got a recipe for virality. Kabosu wasn't just a dog; she was a Meme, a digital artifact that resonated across borders and bandwidths. And she wouldn't be the last.

In 2013, two software engineers, Jackson Palmer and Billy Markus, decided to take a jab at the crypto craze. Bitcoin was all the rage, with its promises of scarcity and digital gold, but Palmer and Markus thought the whole thing was getting too absurd. To highlight this, they created Dogecoin, a cryptocurrency they developed in less than an hour as a satirical middle finger. Instead of Bitcoin's tightly controlled supply, Dogecoin was comically abundant, churning out new coins every second like a malfunctioning slot machine. The logo? You guessed it. A Shiba Inu dog, naturally, with a squinting, quizzical face. It was a joke, a way to mock the speculators who thought crypto was the second coming. But the Internet doesn't care about your intentions. Dogecoin took off, surging 1,000% in its first two weeks to hit $0.0023 per coin. Four years later, in 2017, it pulled another 1,000% run. And then, in 2021, the real insanity kicked in.

Elon Musk, the world's richest person and crypto's most unpredictable figure, posted a single word on what was then Twitter: "Doge." That was all it took. Dogecoin went, well, to the moon, soaring 10,000% between January and May 2021. At its peak, it was worth $85 billion, roughly equivalent to the market capitalization of Boeing at the time. A coin that started as a prank, thrown together by two guys in a spare hour, was now a financial behemoth, more valuable than the world's oldest commercial plane maker. Wall Street rolled its eyes. Venture capitalists smirked into their oat-milk lattes. However, the kids on Reddit, those trading Doge on their phones while watching TikTok, were minting life-changing sums. Dogecoin wasn't just a coin; it was a movement, a rebuke to the suits who thought they controlled the game.

McCann didn't laugh. He studied. Dogecoin wasn't a fluke; it was a signal, a flare shot into the sky of the Internet's new economy. This wasn't about balance sheets or discounted cash flows. This wasn't taught at Harvard Business School. It was about vibes, shared jokes, and collective belief. And dogs, for reasons nobody could fully articulate, were the Internet's favorite currency.

McCann's life had been a masterclass in spotting patterns nobody else could see. Growing up, he'd been a nomad, a kid who had to decipher a new social norm with every new school, every new town. He noticed everything, soaking it up like a sponge. He'd take a mental note on how a certain jacket could make you untouchable in one place but invisible in another, the way a catchphrase could spread like a virus or die on the vine. By the time he was a teenager, he could read a room, or a culture, like a book. He knew who the tastemakers were before they knew it themselves. He could predict which trends would cross state lines and which would stay local. It was a skill honed by necessity, a survival mechanism for a kid who was always the new guy.

That skill carried him into adulthood. After college, he worked at top design agencies, spending hours agonizing over the curve of a font or the shade of a color. He spun records as a DJ, his bald head and chiseled profile a precursor to David Solomon, the Goldman Sachs CEO, who also moonlighted as DJ Sol. He designed clothing lines, invested in startups, and traded markets with the precision of a mathematician. He was as conversant in Kandinsky's color theory as he was in Python's code. He was the kind of guy who could walk into a room full of coders, artists, or traders and hold his own, because he spoke their languages. And when cryptocurrency came along, it was like the universe had built a sandbox just for him.

Crypto was about more than money; it was about culture, technology, and art colliding in a glorious, chaotic mess. Meme coins were the purest distillation of that collision. They didn't need a whitepaper or a killer app. They needed a story, a logo, a vibe. And McCann could spot the winners from a mile away. In August 2020, when Shiba Inu launched on the Ethereum blockchain, he saw the pattern again. Another dog, this one sleeker, more cartoonish, with a fast-food aesthetic and bright yellows and reds that screamed "buy me." The supply? A quadrillion coins, a number so absurd it was almost performance art. The purpose? To go up.

And it did, spectacularly. A $1,000 investment in Shiba Inu in August 2020 was worth $13 million by November 2024. At its peak, Shiba Inu's market cap hit $6 billion, twice the size of Macy's, the department store that had been a fixture of American life for more than a century. Wall Street called it a scam, a bubble, a joke. McCann called it genius.

When BONK appeared in late 2022, McCann didn't blink. It had all the hallmarks of a blue-chip Meme coin, the kind that could go from zero to billions in a heartbeat. A dog logo? Check. Basic utility as a payment for NFTs? Check. Listings on major exchanges like Coinbase? Check. A decentralized autonomous organization (DAO) that lets token holders vote on the coin's future, like shareholders in a digital co-op? Check. And most crucially, it made no sense, which made perfect sense. Younger investors, the ones who'd grown up on Snapchat, TikTok, and Robinhood, didn't give a damn about Warren Buffett's value investing or the efficient market hypothesis. They didn't believe in 401(k)s or the promise of a comfy retirement. They'd seen their parents get crushed by the 2008 financial crisis, watched the gig economy turn jobs into hustles, and decided the American Dream was a rigged game. But a dog with a hat? A coin that could turn $100 into $100,000? That was something they could believe in.

There was another layer to BONK that hooked McCann, something most traders missed. Every major blockchain had its Meme coin, its mascot for the masses. Ethereum had Shiba Inu, the slicker, shinier cousin that rode Doge's coattails to billions. Solana, the fastest and cheapest blockchain in the game, didn't have one. That was a gap, a void, and an opportunity. If Solana was the future, BONK would be its flag-bearer.

McCann dove in headfirst, buying up BONK like a man on a mission. The coin launched with a $28 million market cap, but he knew that was just the starting line. This was asymmetric risk, the kind of bet his firm was named for and the type of trade on which he was all in: big rewards, minimal downside. He pegged BONK for $1 billion, maybe $1.5 billion if the stars aligned. He wasn't just right; he was spectacularly, gloriously, right. BONK didn't stop at $1 billion. It hit $2 billion, and Asymmetric Financial's returns catapulted it into the stratosphere, making it one of the best-performing hedge funds on Wall Street in 2023, according to Bloomberg. The financial press, always late to the party, dubbed McCann the Meme King. He didn't argue with the title. He wore it like a crown.

The success of BONK wasn't just about the coin. It was also about Solana making it all possible. Solana's speed and scalability were the secret sauce, the reason Meme coins like BONK could thrive. It's the crypto version of Apple's App Store: a platform so smooth and versatile that developers could build anything, from games to social networks to, well, cartoon dogs with market caps. BONK's whitepaper didn't mince words: it aimed to be the "community coin of Solana," a currency for NFTs, gaming, and whatever else the Internet dreamed up. And it delivered. BONK became an accepted payment for a slew of NFTs on Solana's ecosystem, giving it just enough utility to keep the skeptics at bay. It also spawned imitators, such as Dogwifhat, another Solana-based Meme coin that followed BONK's playbook and achieved blue-chip status, meaning a market cap exceeding two billion. The pattern was undeniable: dogs plus Internet plus lightning-fast blockchains equaled money.

McCann saw the bigger picture, the one that Wall Street, with its spreadsheets and risk models, couldn't grasp. The Internet was no longer a separate realm; it was converging with the real world, and Meme coins were the bridge. They weren't just assets; they were a way to trade culture, to monetize the intangible. There was no discounted cash flow to crunch, no earnings report to parse. It was about knowing what's cool, what's viral, what's next. "You can't analyze it!" McCann would tell anyone who'd listen. "People love dogs. They share pictures of dogs. It's not supposed to mean anything!" But it did mean something, in its own warped, wonderful way. Meme coins were a rebellion, a way for the little guy, the kid on Reddit, the barista with a Robinhood account, to stick it to the hedge funds and investment banks who'd rigged the system for decades. Most of the time, you'd lose. Nine out of 10 Meme coins were duds, destined to crash and burn. But the one that hit? They were jackpots, life-changing bets that turned pocket change into fortunes.

McCann's genius wasn't just in spotting BONK; it was in understanding the world that made BONK possible. He'd seen the tech world evolve, from the clunky PCs of the '90s to the sleek smartphones of today. He remembered the days when computers could barely handle one program at a time, when opening a spreadsheet and a browser simultaneously was a recipe for a blue screen of death. Then came Intel's Pentium, with its parallel processing, and suddenly the world changed. You could multitask, run multiple threads, and build software that felt alive. Back in the '90s, computers were slow, single-threaded dinosaurs. You could run one program at a time, and if you tried to multitask, you'd crash the system. That one innovation unlocked a tidal wave of creativity, spreadsheets, games, browsers, all running at once. Solana was doing the same for blockchain, processing thousands of transactions in parallel, making it faster and cheaper than Ethereum. McCann had seen this movie before, not in crypto but in tech, and crypto was following the same arc.

Bitcoin was the first mover, the digital equivalent of IBM's Stretch supercomputer from the 1960s, a hulking, expensive marvel that could do one thing well: store value. Ethereum was the next step, like the Apple II, smaller and more versatile, capable of running smart contracts. But Ethereum was slow, clunky, like a single-threaded app struggling to keep up. Solana was the iPhone, fast, lightweight, and fun, capable of juggling thousands of transactions at once. It was a platform for the future.

McCann saw the parallel instantly. "Ethereum's cool; it was the first smart contract platform, but it's flawed," he'd tell clients. "It's slow, it's expensive, it's like trying to run a marathon in flip-flops. Solana is different. They're doing parallel computing for blockchain.

You don't need a PhD to see that's going to work." He wasn't wrong. Solana's architecture, with its ability to process transactions in parallel, made it the go-to platform for developers building everything from DeFi apps to NFT marketplaces to, yes, Meme coins. And BONK was the perfect proof of concept, a coin that captured the Internet's love for dogs and Solana's technical wizardry in one tidy package.

Of course, BONK's rise wasn't without its critics. Traditional finance types, the ones who'd spent their careers at Goldman Sachs or Morgan Stanley, called it a scam, a Ponzi scheme, a bubble waiting to pop. They weren't entirely wrong. Meme coins were volatile, speculative, and often devoid of intrinsic value. But that was the point. Value, as McCann knew, wasn't about fundamentals; it was about belief. The critics missed that. They saw a dog logo and scoffed because they couldn't see the culture behind it. They couldn't see the kids on Discord, the communities on Reddit, the TikTok videos hyping BONK to the moon. They couldn't see the DAO, the decentralized organization that gave BONK holders a say in its future, turning them into digital shareholders. They couldn't see the forest for the trees.

McCann could. He'd spent his life studying the forest, mapping its trails, learning its rhythms. He knew that culture wasn't just noise; it was a signal, a force that could move markets faster than any earnings report. He'd seen it in high school, when a pair of Air Jordans could make you a god. He'd seen it in design when a font choice could make or break a brand. He'd seen it in crypto, when a tweet from Elon Musk could send a coin into orbit. And he saw it in BONK, a coin that was less about utility and more about joy and about the thrill of being part of something bigger, something absurd, something that made the suits on Wall Street clutch their pearls, and something that could defy gravity.

The BONK phenomenon didn't stop with BONK. It sparked a wave of imitators, each trying to capture the same magic. Dogwifhat, another Solana-based Meme coin, was the most successful, hitting blue-chip status with a market cap that rivaled BONK's. The pattern was now a playbook: find a cute dog, slap it on a coin, launch it on Solana, and watch the Internet do the rest. But McCann knew it wasn't that simple. The Internet was fickle. It could love you one day and ghost you the next. For every Dogecoin or Shiba Inu, there were dozens of duds, coins that launched with fanfare and fizzled into obscurity. The difference was in the details, the logo, the community, and the timing. BONK had nailed it, with its fast-food aesthetic, its NFT utility, and its Solana backbone. It was a perfect storm, and McCann had ridden it like a pro.

BONK worked when so many others failed in part because of Solana, no question. The blockchain's speed and low fees made it the ideal playground for Meme coins, just as the iPhone's ecosystem made it possible for apps like Instagram and Uber to take over the world. Part of it was the DAO, which gave BONK a veneer of legitimacy. Part of it was the Internet itself, with its endless hunger for novelty and community. However, the most significant aspect, the one that McCann kept coming back to, was the dogs. There was something about dogs, such as Snoopy, Lassie, and Kabosu, that tapped into a universal longing. They were loyal, they were funny, they were us. And when you put a dog on a coin, you weren't just selling a token; you were selling a feeling.

By the end of 2023, McCann was a legend, the Meme King who'd turned a cartoon dog into a $2 billion empire. Asymmetric Financial was the talk of the industry, a hedge fund that had outsmarted the quants and the algos by betting on the Internet's weirdest corner. But McCann wasn't resting on his laurels. He was already looking for the next pattern, the next signal in the noise. The Internet was evolving, and so was crypto. Solana was just the beginning; there were new blockchains, new coins, and new Memes waiting to be born. And McCann, with his designer's eye, his trader's instincts, and his nomad's intuition, was ready to find them.

Now I'm not advocating for you to go out and buy Meme coins. That is not my game and never has been. However, I think the Meme craze illustrates, as clearly as possible, why the Solana network has value. It's fast and inexpensive, and its technology enables users to tap into their creative instincts to create and trade coins. I believe Solana allows guys like McCann to express and monetize their cultural instincts. Does it seem silly to some? Maybe. Perhaps, but it's no sillier than saying the Nasdaq was a joke because Petsdotcom busted out in 2001. That same network, the Nasdaq, was also home to Amazon and Microsoft, two companies that transformed how we live and do business today. Solana will do the same for the companies and commerce of the future.

McCann understood that, and that's why he was able to monetize his cultural genius. It wasn't just about the money. Sure, the money was nice, great even. But what drove him was the puzzle, the challenge of decoding the Internet's chaotic heartbeat. "It's like the Supreme Court and pornography," he'd later tell investors. "I can't define it, but I know it when I see it." And when he saw BONK's cartoon dog, he knew. He saw the future, not in a crystal ball but in a logo, a silly, absurd, perfect logo that captured everything the Internet was and everything it could be.

Chapter 9

Shining a Light on Solana: How to Buy, Borrow, and Build

O kay, I've told you about this amazing network. I've described some of the magical things it can do. And I've given you an inside glimpse into the people animating this crazy community of coins and charisma. Now I'm going to show you how you can participate, too. Get ready, because I'm going to teach you how to really harness the power of this amazing network.

Your introduction to Solana's world starts with buying SOL, Solana's native token. As we detailed before, SOL is the gas that powers everything on the Solana network. It's what you use to pay tiny fees for transactions, interact with apps, or even stake to earn rewards. And if it goes up, you'll make money. Buying SOL is as easy as shopping online. Solana started by creating 500 million SOL coins. Unlike Bitcoin, which has a strict limit of 21 million coins, Solana doesn't have a fixed cap, but the network carefully controls how many new coins are made. To prevent too many coins from flooding the system, Solana reduces the number of coins over time, balancing out the new ones created. It's like trimming a plant to keep it healthy. This setup ensures the network stays sustainable without growing out of control.

The easiest way to buy SOL is to go to a crypto exchange, like Coinbase or Kraken, which are designed to look and feel like your average online broker. There's a bid-ask spread. Charts. Account positions. They're probably the most user friendly of all the online crypto brokers. You can also buy crypto through leading online brokers like Robinhood or Interactive Brokers. You sign up like you would on any broker dealer: you enter your email, create a password, and verify your identity. Once your account is ready, you can deposit dollars from your bank account or credit card and use them to buy SOL. The process is simple. Search for SOL, enter the amount you want to buy, and confirm. In minutes, you'll see SOL in your Coinbase wallet. Welcome to the world of Solana.

So, what role should Solana play in your portfolio? Every investor is different, and you should consult your financial advisor before making any moves. Having said that, I feel Solana should be a substantial part of your portfolio. For all the reasons I've laid out in this book, I believe crypto should play a role in any well-balanced portfolio. It's an asset class, just like stocks or bonds. A portfolio without crypto is not a balanced portfolio. It should be a core holding, like fixed income or equities. If you're new to the space and want to start small, maybe allocate 5% of your overall portfolio to crypto. Of that 5%, 2% should be in Solana and the rest in Bitcoin. Now, you might think that is a lot, but it really isn't. Sure, it would hurt if crypto went to zero, but it won't, just like the S&P 500 won't go to zero. But if crypto continues on its path, that 5% allocation could change your life. Just imagine had you bought Bitcoin at the year-to-date highs over the past 10 years. Despite all the crashes, you'd still be up, significantly. If you bought $5,000 worth of Bitcoin when it first topped $20,000 in 2018, you are sitting on $25,000 today. That number will only grow as Bitcoin continues to rise. Even if you sold along the way, as any disciplined investor should, you'd still have made a killing. Now, some of you might be saying, "I can't risk that type of money." I get it. Investing, particularly in volatile assets, can be intimidating. But imagine if you avoided the Nasdaq because Amazon or Tesla have experienced multiple drawdowns of 70%. New asset classes are challenging to predict and even more difficult to price on a short-term basis. But that must not stop you.

I am in the more aggressive camp. I believe a minimum of 10% of your portfolio should be allocated to crypto. Losing 10% will crush your soul, but it won't kill you. And if you're buying into one of the greatest asset classes around, you're going look back one day with regret that you didn't buy more. Anything less than 10% won't provide the real benefits of ownership. Imagine if you had allocated 10% of your portfolio to blue-chip crypto assets a decade ago, when Bitcoin was just over $200 and everyone was calling it a bubble or worse? You'd have generational wealth. Imagine going back 10 or 15 years and having the chance to buy Apple or Netflix, when short sellers were howling about valuations and tech bubbles. Of course, it wasn't. Those companies were creating and destroying entire industries. Crypto is doing the same. I recall a story the great Michael Saylor once told me. In 2010, Saylor bought $50 million worth of the so-called FANG stocks (Facebook, Apple, Netflix, and Google). He recognized their transformative power and bought accordingly. He quickly turned it into $500 million and took profits. The move made him a small fortune, but instead of rejoicing, Saylor felt regret.

"It was one of the biggest mistakes I ever made," Saylor told me over lunch about his decision to cash out.

I was dumbfounded. What could he have possibly meant? A 10-bagger is the investment equivalent of Haley's Comet; they come once in a lifetime. And he was sad about this?

"You don't have enough money, Michael? Are you lacking?" I jokingly asked.

"It's not the money. It's the principle," Saylor instantly replied.

He went on to explain that he didn't regret the small fortune he made. He didn't even regret that he didn't make more. Saylor had more money than he knew what to do with. What he really regretted was that he turned his back on an investment principle that, until he made all that money, didn't even know existed.

"If you find a dominant investment, Anthony, don't just buy it," Saylor said. "You buy it and then buy it some more! And then, just when you think you can't buy any more, you figure out a way to buy just a touch more, and then you go on X and incessantly post about it!"

We laughed, but the point could not be more serious: once-in-a-lifetime investments come around only once in a lifetime, if you're lucky. And when they do, never turn your back. When Saylor loaded up on FANG, he wasn't just buying tech stocks; he was actually buying slivers of change-agents, particles of progress that would transform society and profoundly change his portfolio. If you ever get a chance to invest in something like that, don't look back. Don't go small. Go big. Go bold. So, when Bitcoin came around, Saylor didn't make the same mistake. He bought aggressively and then proceeded to buy even more aggressively. And then, true to his world, he went on social media and posted about it. Keep in mind that he's a Bitcoin maximalist, which means he believes the most significant risk in owning Bitcoin is not owning more. He'd rather own too much and stomach the volatility than own too little and miss out on what he sees as a can't-miss trade. Most people don't share this view, and that's understandable. But, if you do get the chance to invest in a transformative technology, embrace it with two arms. Don't look back. You don't have to be a maximalist, but you may have to move outside your comfort zone. Of course, everyone should consult with their financial advisors, but for my money, when a generational trade presents itself, it's foolish not to embrace it in a meaningful way.

Fortunately, I got that chance with Bitcoin. It was the greatest trade I've ever made in my decade on Wall Street. It was an investment that saved my firm, changed my perspective on life, and opened a whole new world for me. I was lucky that I had such great ambassadors to the world of the coin. Peter Brigger, Mike Novogratz, and my partner Brett Messing were instrumental in opening my eyes. We had a lot on the line. Transitioning from a traditional asset manager to a Bitcoin firm was not a layup. There were critics, many of whom were our customers. But we stayed the course, and we were rewarded. Handsomely.

Solana is that second great investment. Will it be as good as Bitcoin was? Who knows? But its transformative technology is opening up the world of DeFi in ways that sound like science fiction. The activities on the network are truly astounding, the very vision of a decentralized financial world once thought unimaginable. And here's the best part: it's only five years old. Just think what will be built on the network in the years to come, when an even greater number of talented programmers flock to the platform. Think of the many different activities you'll be able to perform. If you believe in programmable money, if you believe in the future of web 3.0, if you believe in DeFi, then Solana should be a core holding in your crypto portfolio—minimum 2% but certainly a much greater percentage of your overall portfolio.

At the time of this writing, spot Solana ETFs do not exist on U.S. exchanges as they do for Bitcoin or Ethereum. Novogratz's Galaxy does sponsor a spot Solana ETF, but that trades on the Canadian exchanges. An application is pending with the SEC, and I suspect it's only a matter of time before the agency clears the way for spot Solana ETFs to trade in the United States. That should unlock a torrent of potential buying, as both professional and retail investors will find an easier on-ramp to the Solana freight train. In the meantime, U.S. investors can consider ETFs that track Solana futures contracts, some of which even offer leverage bets on the underlying asset. These are bought just like stocks through your online broker. There's even a Grayscale Solana Trust, which trades OTC. Since it's a trust and not an ETF, it's unable to redeem or issue shares, which can lead it to trade at either a discount or a premium to its net asset value. For more sophisticated investors, Solana futures contracts are available for trading on the Chicago Mercantile Exchange. The low margin requirements make futures a smart way to make a leveraged bet on a particular asset, and that is also true for Solana. Personally, I'm not a huge fan of retail traders using futures to express an investment thesis on crypto. There are periods, particularly over the weekend, when futures do not trade, limiting your ability to get in and out of trades. Managing expirations and rolling contracts adds a measure of difficulty that can be challenging for even seasoned professional traders. If you're looking for exposure to a crypto asset, just buy the asset. No need to get cute with futures unless you're a sophisticated investor, in which case, they are a great tool.

Several leveraged ETFs provide exposure to Solana through the futures market. The fees are a little high for my taste, and again, I always believe in buying the underlying asset. The Grayscale Solana Trust (GSOL) trades on the over-the-counter market, providing indirect exposure. But because it's a trust and not a true ETF, it may trade at a premium or discount to SOL's price due to its inability to create or redeem outstanding shares. Its application to become an EFT is pending with the SEC.

I like not to overthink things and keep them simple. Just buy the coin SOL. Anything that increases from $1 to $150 in five years is likely not going to continue rising. As the community and network continue to grow and the number of applications increases, SOL coins are likely to benefit and continue to rise. But if you just bought SOL coins, you'd be missing out on all the wonderful things the Solana network offers. You borrow, lend, and even create your own network that pays you to explore. It's magical, like something out of a science fiction film. Let me walk you through some of it.

Let's say you're out for dinner and you owe your friend $20. Instead of using cash or a bank app, you decide to send them $20 directly. Sending tokens is fun and easy and will allow you to really explore how crypto works. To get started, you'll need a Solana wallet app, like Phantom or Solfare. Download the app, create a wallet, and transfer your SOL from your broker or bank to your wallet. Now, open your wallet app. You'll see your SOL balance, which you'll use to pay a tiny "gas" fee, a small amount to cover the cost of processing your transaction on the Solana network. Your friend gives you their public key, which is like their wallet's address. You can think of it as their email for crypto. You enter their public key, type in $20 worth of SOL, and hit Send. In just a few seconds, your friend gets a notification that the SOL is in their wallet.

The process seems simple, but there's actually a lot happening behind the scenes. When you hit Send, you "sign" the transaction with your private key, a secret code that proves it's really you sending the money. Your private key is super important; never share it with anyone. Treat it like you would your ATM PIN code. Meanwhile, Solana's network of computers verifies the transaction to ensure everything adds up. Once approved, the transaction is added to the blockchain. This all happens in seconds, with no bank or middleman involved. It's fast, it's secure, and it feels like you've just unlocked a superpower.

Now that you've sent money, let's try something more exciting: lending your SOL to earn interest. This is where Solana's many DeFi apps come in. DeFi is similar to traditional finance in that it involves activities that require loans or savings accounts, but these are executed by code, not banks. It's one of the coolest parts of Solana. Now you might be thinking, "Mooch, it's one thing to buy SOL on Coinbase. Quite another to lend it out like some prime broker." But I'm here to tell you it's easier than you might think.

First, find a DeFi lending protocol on the Solana blockchain, like MarginFi or Drift. These protocols act as the middleman, but it's not a traditional bank. It's just simple code, and here's how it works. You deposit your SOL into the protocol, which tracks its value. Now, you can lend your SOL directly and earn interest as a reward. It's like lending SOL to a friend who pays you back with a little extra, except the protocol handles everything automatically. The terms are transparent, and the blockchain ensures no one can cheat.

Now let's flip it around. What if you want to borrow SOL instead? That's easy, too. You deposit SOL as collateral, agree to the protocol's terms, and receive SOL in your wallet. Instead of buying, you could lend it out instead, for a small fee of course. When you're ready to get your SOL collateral back, you repay the borrowed SOL plus a small amount of interest, and your collateral is returned. Now, many people choose to borrow and lend against stablecoins because they are more, well, stable in price. SOL's inherent volatility makes it a little trickier than pegging it to a stablecoin.

However, the real beauty of all this lies in the transparency. With DeFi, you can see exactly how much you're earning or paying, and the code ensures everything happens as it should. It's a new way to manage money, and Solana's speed makes it smooth and fun, and its design makes it super cheap, which makes borrowing and lending more profitable. Just be careful. As with any speculative behavior, always use trusted protocols, and don't lend or borrow more than you're comfortable with.

Okay, we've bought, borrowed, and lent SOL coins. Now let's get crazy and really harness the power of the network. We talked earlier about Meme King Joe McCann and the inherent beauty of Meme coin culture. Maybe it's time to launch your own coin. It's actually easier than you think.

On other blockchains, creating a token is risky because anyone can write code with hidden tricks. Solana addresses this issue with its Solana Program Library (SPL), a set of trusted rules for creating tokens. Every SPL token follows the same safe standards, so you don't have to worry about scams or errors. It's like using a particular and detailed recipe from a trusted cookbook. You know it'll turn out right.

So, to create your coin, you can use a platform like Pump.fun, a beginner-friendly tool built on Solana. When you visit the site, connect it to your Solana wallet. First, pick a name. For our purposes, let's call it Dogcoin and include a description. With a few clicks, you've launched your coin, and it's live on the Solana blockchain. It's literally that easy! But for people to trade your coin, you need liquidity, or a number of people willing to buy or sell it. This is where a bonding curve comes in. Think of a bonding curve as a mathematical formula that acts as a market maker. It sets a starting price for your coin. If people buy it, the price of the coin goes up. If they sell it, the price goes down, but the curve keeps the market active. For example, if no one buys Dogcoin, its value stays at zero. But if someone buys a few tokens, the curve adjusts the price upward, encouraging others to join in. Your coin is now tradable, and you've just created something new on the Solana network. Creating a coin is exciting, but it's not a get-rich-quick scheme. Many new tokens don't gain traction, so do your research and start small.

Of course, buying, selling, lending, and creating coins on the Solana network is just one of many possibilities. We talked about the Apes and digital collectables, and there's no reason you can't participate in this market, too.

You can buy NFTs using SOL or USDC. Each NFT is stored on the blockchain. It's like owning a rare baseball card, but because they're digital, unlike baseball cards, they can't be faked, damaged, or lost. And, you can just trade them instantly online, no one has to get on eBay or go to a physical store.

To get started, connect your Solana wallet to an NFT marketplace like Magic Eden. Once connected, you can begin to buy and sell various NFTs just like you would a coin or stock. Each NFT is stored on Solana's blockchain, which validates the token and safely stores it. The process is no different from buying collectables online. When you find an NFT you love, maybe it's something with an Ape or a Dog, just click the Buy button. After a tiny transaction fee, your wallet will be debited, and the

NFT will be yours, stored safely on the Solana Blockchain. Fast. Cheap. Fun.

You can keep your NFT, show it off in digital galleries, or sell it later on Magic Eden if its value rises or falls. But be smart. Approach buying an NFT like you would any collectible or piece of art. Do research. Ask yourself who the NFT's creator is. How have their previous NFTs performed? What community are they targeting? Many NFTs lose value, so like Meme coins, don't risk a lot. Start with a small amount you don't mind losing. As you start trading more, you'll get a better feel for the technology and the vibrant (and at times over-the-top) creator community. Check out various chat groups on Reddit and Discord to learn about new projects and trends. Anyone who loves collectables will love buying and selling NFTs. It's fun. It's creative, and you might make a lot of money along the way.

But there's even more. There are a number of apps and games that allow you to earn money simply by engaging with the platform. Some apps let you earn SOL tokens by playing video games on the network. There's even an app called Stepn that pays you to walk. Others will pay you to take surveys. Once you start participating, you'll start to see SOL awarded in your wallet. As with anything, check out the app's reputation before engaging with it. As with the NFTs or any activity on the Solana network, start small to establish a comfort zone. Earning tokens through various apps is a fun way to turn a hobby into a money-making endeavor. Solana's official home page at solana.com is a great educational resource.

The broader point here is that Solana makes the blockchain intuitive and fun, much like the iPhone did two decades ago. You'll be shocked by all the things you can do, even if you don't consider yourself a tech-savvy person, which, as anyone who knows me knows, I am not. But you'll get there. Prior to the iPhone, did you think you could with the touch of a virtual button, dit and upload PDFs, book travel tickets, or explore the web? But the interface and browser were revelations that turned everyone, young and old alike, into experts. It's the same thing with Solana. It's an easy, inexpensive, and fast network that enables you to perform tasks and earn money in ways you never thought possible.

Of course, you'd just be scratching the surface of Solana's potential if all you did was launch and trade MEMEcoins on the network. Those activities may grab headlines and win attention, but it's not what makes the network a crypto jewel. It would be the equivalent of using an iPhone solely for texting and taking occasional pictures; you would be missing out on so much. The real beauty of the iPhone is the world it opens up. Through its various apps, you can stream movies, bank, book vacations, compose complicated documents, and hold team meetings while sitting on a beach. It's magic, and in a lot of ways, Solana is no different. It's a network that can perform magic. Through its unparalleled technology and design, it's a platform that brings Web 3.0 to life. Yakovenko and his partners didn't simply create another blockchain; they made a world of possibility, the type of world that shocks you with its limitless potential. Because Solana's founders focused so intently on speed, scalability, and usability, the platform has become more than a destination for innovation; it's home to some of the most imaginative and transformative technology in the world. It may sound hyperbolic, but it's not, and it's why I remain so bullish on this network and the coin that powers it. Three applications embody Solana's potential: Helium, a decentralized 5G network that lets anyone become a telecom provider; Hivemapper, a community-driven mapping platform challenging Google's dominance; and BlackRock's BUIDL, a tokenized money market fund that brings Wall Street onto the blockchain. These weren't just experimental new applications; they are concrete examples of industries rethinking their foundations and how they interact with customers. To understand Solana's rise, you have to understand each for both their audacity and their creativity in accessing the blockchain to harness Solana's magic.

Helium: The Internet That's Yours

Okay, this is going to blow your mind. Most people think of cellular service as a centralized, individual service. But thanks to the Solana network, that notion is a thing of the past. Let me explain it in simple terms. Imagine a lemonade stand, but not just one kid selling drinks. Picture a whole neighborhood where every kid has got their own stand, and they're all sharing the lemons, sugar, and cash they make. When you buy a cup from one stand, the money gets split up instantly among all the kids, so they're motivated to keep pouring drinks and inviting more friends to join. Now, swap lemonade for super-fast 5G Internet, and that's how Helium works. It's like a giant, shared Wi-Fi network that anyone can help build and use, without needing big companies like Verizon or AT&T. You just grab a little gadget called a hotspot, plug it in at home, and instantly you're part of a worldwide Internet network. For about $20 a month, you get 5G that works in tons of places, from your street to cities across the globe. Plus, you can earn a little money for sharing your hotspot's signal all run on the Solana blockchain. I know what you're thinking: what does the blockchain have to do with talking on a cell phone? Allow me to explain.

Back in 2013, three guys, Amir Haleem, Shawn Fanning, and Marc Nijdam, decided to shake things up. Haleem is from Pakistan, where he grew up dealing with spotty electricity and Internet connections, so he became really interested in building systems that didn't crash and could function with limited infrastructure. He's a gamer at heart, which helped him make Helium fast and reliable. Fanning was the less famous Shawn to create Napster. Yes, that Napster, the music-sharing app from way back that brought Tower Records to its knees and was founded by one Sean Parker, who went on to Facebook and Spotify. The latter Shawn, Shawn Fanning, is from Massachusetts and loves finding ways to break down old systems, such as monopolistic record companies and big telecom giants that charge way too much. In short, he likes to disrupt The System, which makes him perfect for crypto. Nijdam was raised in the Netherlands and spent many years at tech giant Cisco, where he worked on various designs and applications for data connectivity. These three started Helium in San Francisco with a wild idea: crowdsource the functionality of the Internet. At first, they focused on something called the Internet of Things, a fancy term for stuff like smart thermostats or sensors that talk to each other over long distances. By 2019, they had thousands of hotspots out there, helping things like pet trackers or farm sensors send data. But that was a small market, and their tech was starting to feel slow. Then 5G came along, which supercharged the Internet and gave cell phones and laptops the equivalent of steroids. With such power, hot spots could be the next cell towers. It was a big leap, but they went for it; however, there was a small problem. They needed a really fast tech platform that could handle thousands of transactions every second without costing a fortune. Enter Solana; in 2021, Helium jumped on the Solana train, and suddenly everything clicked. Hotspots could share data instantly, people could pay for the Internet easily, and the network could grow without slowing down. By 2025, Helium had 400,000 hotspots in 180 countries, helping millions of people. I've talked to people who are pretty techy, and they are blown away by the power of this product. In fact, many folks I know have switched their phones to Helium from Verizon. Don't be surprised if you hear folks begin to say Helium is their cell provider.

Some very big and important investors are already saying that. In 2019, both Union Square Ventures and Samani's Multicoin, who loved the idea of a network that rewards participants for helping out, invested in the company. When Helium shifted to 5G in 2021, Andreessen Horowitz, a huge venture capital firm, led a $111 million round, with others like Ribbit Capital and 10T Holdings joining in. Tiger Global also hopped on in 2022, valuing

Helium at $1.2 billion. At one point in 2025, Helium's valuation touched $2 billion, and their token, HNT, traded as high as $5 each, which validates customers' belief in the network.

Best of all, while it sounds complicated, it's actually pretty easy to use. If a luddite from Portchester Long Island can work it, I suspect you can, too. It's effectively like setting up your own hotspot. A hotspot is a little box, about the size of a Wi-Fi router, that you buy for $300 to $500. You plug that hotspot into your Internet router, connect it to power, and use a phone app to get it going. It sends out signals that power your phone's Internet. These hotspots talk to each other, creating a big, connected web of Internet coverage, almost like validators on the blockchain. And like a blockchain, it uses a consensus mechanism to make sure everyone's hotspot is doing its job. In Helium's case, it uses something called "proof of coverage." It's like a game where hotspots check in with each other to prove they're working and covering their area. If your hotspot passes the test, you earn HNT tokens, which are just like digital coins. Solana makes this happen super-fast, so there's no waiting around.

When someone uses your hotspot's Internet, for example, your neighbor streams a video, they pay with something called "data credits," which are tied to the U.S. dollar, so their value remains stable. These credits are converted into HNT, and you receive a share based on the amount of Internet you provided. Say your hotspot handles 1GB of data; you'll earn a bit of HNT for that. Solana keeps fees minimal, so you retain most of what you earn. You manage all this through Helium's app, which works with Solana to keep things simple. The best part? Helium is open to everyone. Companies compete to make better, cheaper hotspots, so they're getting more affordable by the day. The network can also add new technologies, such as Wi-Fi or even satellite signals, so it continues to grow and improve. It allows you to harness the power of the blockchain to become a telecom titan or, at the very least, a telecom provider.

Helium is awesome, but of course, it's not flawless. Setting up a hotspot can be a hassle. Some super-rural spots still lack coverage, and HNT, the network's token, can fluctuate in price, which makes some people nervous. A few countries are also considering rules to limit networks like Helium, as they worry about losing control. However, Helium's open setup means companies continue to develop better hotspots, and Solana's low costs mean it's likely to grow as more people look to turn a liability like your phone bill into an asset that can actually generate income. Big telecom companies have spotty service in rural areas, as anyone who's ever gone camping can attest, and that's likely not going to change for sparsely populated areas. But Helium solves this by letting people build their own Internet. With 400,000 hotspots and counting, Helium is turning the Internet into something we all share, one hotspot at a time, and potentially profit from.

But that's just scraping the surface of Solana's potential.

Hivemapper: Mapping the World, One Drive at a Time

Imagine a jigsaw puzzle the size of the planet, with billions of pieces scattered across cities, deserts, and mountain passes. Now picture thousands of drivers, from taxi drivers in Mumbai to delivery workers in São Paulo to commuters in Chicago, each adding a piece to the puzzle every time they hit the road. Each piece is a snapshot: a newly paved street, a faded stop sign, a traffic jam caused by a sudden accident. These fragments, captured by dashcams and uploaded to a decentralized network, are stitched together into a living, breathing map of the world. That's precisely what Hivemapper is doing; it is a Solana-based platform that crowdsources maps to challenge Google's own map empire, one car at a time. Drivers mount a dashcam, record their routes, and upload the data to Hivemapper's network. Solana's blockchain processes it, rewards contributors with tokens called HONEY, and builds a map that's fresher, more accurate, and more open than anything Google or other tech titans currently offer. It's like Wikipedia for maps, powered by Solana's efficiency and animated by a global community of everyday drivers like you and me.

Hivemapper was founded in 2015 by Ariel Seidman, a mapping obsessive with a Silicon Valley pedigree and a vision to democratize the map-making process. Seidman was born in Tel Aviv, Israel, in 1970, and he grew up in a city where navigating narrow streets and bustling markets required an intimate and encyclopedic knowledge of roads and intersections. His family immigrated to the United States when he was a teenager, settling in Palo Alto, California, during the heart of the tech boom. Seidman's early fascination with maps, born and hardened from a childhood spent wandering the winding streets of Tel Aviv's labyrinthine neighborhoods, blossomed into a career in technology. A wiry marathon runner with a sharp intellect and a relentless drive, Seidman studied computer science at Stanford University, where he was captivated by the potential of digital mapping to transform how people interact with the world.

Seidman's professional journey took him to Yahoo in the early 2000s, where he worked on one of the Internet's first consumer mapping platforms. Yahoo Maps, though rudimentary compared to today's standards, was a revelation at the time, offering turn-by-turn directions and satellite views to millions. Seidman saw the power of maps to connect people to places but was frustrated by the slow pace of centralized data collection. Later, he joined Apple to work on its ambitious but troubled mapping app, launched in 2012 to compete with Google Maps. Apple's Maps debut was a public relations disaster, riddled with errors like mislabeled landmarks and distorted roads. The experience left Seidman disillusioned with top-down approaches to mapping. He began to dream of a system where maps weren't built by corporations with billion-dollar budgets but by the very individuals who used them: drivers, cyclists, and pedestrians who knew their streets better than any satellite could.

Seidman's inspiration for Hivemapper came from a blend of frustration and optimism. He saw how Google Maps dominated the industry through sheer scale, powered by fleets of Street View cars, satellites orbiting the Earth, and billions in the bank. But Google's approach had flaws, in his view. Its data was often stale, with new roads or construction updates taking months to appear. Its platform was a walled garden, tightly controlled and inaccessible to developers who wanted to build custom applications on top of the existing platform. Seidman believed a decentralized model could outmaneuver the giants by leveraging the collective power of millions of drivers. They would in effect become the customers and custodians of the map, just like nodes work to ensure the integrity of a blockchain. He envisioned a network where anyone with a car and a dashcam could contribute to a global map, earning rewards for their efforts. In 2015, he founded Hivemapper in San Francisco, betting that crowdsourcing and blockchain technology could converge and disrupt the mapping industry.

The early years were a grind. Hivemapper's first dashcam, a bulky prototype, was expensive to produce and cumbersome to install. Adoption was slow, as drivers were hesitant to invest in unproven technology. Processing the massive volumes of video data required for mapping was another hurdle, with cloud computing costs eating into the company's budget. Seidman's team initially built a custom blockchain to handle transactions and data verification, but it struggled to scale under the weight of huge data loads. By 2020, Hivemapper was on the brink of failure, with dwindling funds and a small user base. Seidman, however, refused to give up. He spent late nights poring over technical papers and meeting with blockchain experts, searching for a solution.

The turning point came in 2022 when Hivemapper migrated to Solana, whose speed and low costs were exactly what he needed to scale effectively. By using Solana, Siedman could now process millions of data points, from images to GPS coordinates to road conditions, in just seconds, enabling Hivemapper to handle the deluge of dashcam footage. Its low fees, often less than a penny per transaction, meant drivers could earn HONEY tokens for every mile driven, even on short commutes. The switch to Solana supercharged Hivemapper's growth. By May 2025, the platform had attracted 50,000 drivers across 70 countries, mapping everything from Tokyo's neon-lit alleys to the dusty backroads of rural India. Hivemapper's map was no longer a proof of concept; it was a viable alternative to Google Maps, with a community-driven ethos and a blockchain backbone. And best of all, if your life involves constant driving, you're now able to get paid for that burden. Suddenly, 405 traffic isn't so bad. You're now able to get paid for your commute.

The money is always nice, but the real beauty is the map itself. Through the Hivemapper app, drivers stitch together a city's streets, which are updated in near real time. A new bike lane here, a temporary road closure there. . .each data point updates and brings the map to life, providing a tremendous amount of real-world usefulness. You get and you give the very latest information and get paid to do so. Driving to work can now become a side hustle. Google Maps, for all its polish and global reach, is a behemoth with inherent limitations. Its data collection relies on a combination of satellite imagery, Street View cars, and user reports, a process that can lag months behind real-world changes. A new roundabout in a small town, a bridge closed for repairs, or a pop-up market blocking a street might not appear on Google Maps until long after drivers need the information. Hivemapper, by contrast, delivers near-real-time updates, thanks to its army of dashcam-equipped drivers. For industries such as autonomous vehicles, ride-sharing, or urban planning, where up-to-date maps are crucial, Hivemapper's timeliness will likely become even more valuable.

Another key advantage is openness. Google Maps is a walled garden, with its data tightly controlled and accessible only through

Google's APIs, which come with steep licensing fees. Hivemapper's maps, built on Solana's blockchain, are open to developers, enabling an ecosystem of third-party applications. Cyclists can use Hivemapper's data to find bike-friendly routes. Urban planners can analyze traffic patterns, and small businesses can integrate real-time road conditions into their delivery systems. You're an owner, contributing to a resource that benefits everyone. It basically turns the role of a commuter into a node on the blockchain, and just like a node, you're rewarded for the work. This openness fosters innovation and ensures that Hivemapper's maps serve a wide range of needs, from individual drivers to multinational corporations.

Cost is another area where Hivemapper shines. Google's mapping operations are staggeringly expensive, requiring fleets of vehicles, satellite contracts, and massive data centers. These hidden costs are passed on to users through advertising and subscriptions, to say nothing of how your data might be used. Hivemapper, by contrast, leverages the existing infrastructure of drivers' cars and Solana's low-cost blockchain. Uploading a gigabyte of dashcam footage costs pennies, ensuring that contributors keep most of their earnings. For businesses, Hivemapper's maps are a bargain, offering high-quality, real-time data at a fraction of the cost of Google's. This cost-efficiency makes Hivemapper an attractive option for startups and small businesses.

Of course, Hivemapper isn't perfect. Coverage remains spotty in rural areas, where fewer drivers mean less data. The AI that processes dashcam footage, while sophisticated, can struggle with complex scenes, like a detour sign obscured by a storm. The platform is addressing these issues, with enhancements to its AI and a focus on recruiting drivers in underserved regions. Powering it all is Solana's speed, which ensures Hivemapper can handle growth, even as the number of contributors swells into the hundreds of thousands.

Like Helium, Hivemapper is not just mapping the world; it's proving a larger, more important point: that decentralized systems can outpace centralized ones and disrupt the disruptors. Hivemapper is doing to Google Maps what Google did to the Thomas Guide 20 years ago—render it moot (and yes, I'm old enough to say I used the Thomas Guide). Ariel Seidman's vision, a map built by the people, for the people, is coming to life, one drive at a time, and it's doing so on the strength and speed of the Solana network.

BlackRock BUIDL on Solana

In March 2025, something big happened in the world of money. BlackRock, the $11.6 trillion asset management behemoth, launched a new kind of beast: the BlackRock USD Institutional Digital Liquidity Fund, or BUIDL for short. BUIDL is a bridge between the slow, suit-and-tie world of Wall Street and the lightning-fast, code-driven universe of crypto, and you can get in on it, whether you're new to crypto or a long-time Wall Street investor.

And driving it all was the company's legendary CEO, Lawrence Fink, a Wall Street icon whose influence extends well beyond any particular market. Fink initially dismissed Bitcoin in 2017 as a speculative tool for illicit deals. He derisively referred to it as an "index for money laundering." But by 2024, his tune changed. He began to embrace the coin, seeing blockchain's potential to streamline finance, make transactions faster, and lower costs to consumers. It's a shift I deeply admire for its intellectual humility. Most smart, rich guys refuse to admit when they're wrong. But Fink is different. He pivoted and became one of the industry's most respected ambassadors, and when the SEC approved Bitcoin ETFs, Fink championed cryptocurrencies on CNBC. BlackRock's Bitcoin ETF debuted in January 2024, amassing $40 billion, the largest ETF launch ever, signaling both institutional and individual demand for crypto. But Fink had a broader vision that extended beyond simple ETF investments. He wanted to tokenize all assets, including cash, bonds, stocks, and art, aimed to make finance as seamless as email. The culminating result was BUIDL.

In March 2024, just months after the smashing success of its Bitcoin ETF, BlackRock partnered with Securitize, a company specializing in turning traditional assets into digital tokens, to launch BUIDL. At its core, BUIDL is a money market fund, a safe place where big players like hedge funds or corporations can park their cash to earn a little interest. Think of it as a super-secure savings account that invests in safe but boring and reliable things like Treasury bills. Traditional money market funds are slow, open only during business hours, and stuck in paperwork. BUIDL changed all that. Your share of the fund is a digital token, worth $1 each, backed by BlackRock's portfolio of cash and Treasuries. You earn interest every day, paid monthly as new tokens to your crypto wallet, and you can trade these tokens anytime, anywhere.

Why is this a big deal for you? If you're holding crypto like SOL or USDC, you've probably noticed a problem: your money just sits there, not earning anything. Stablecoins like USDC keep your cash steady, but they don't pay interest. Sending it to a bank means converting to dollars, paying fees, and waiting days—not exactly an ideal timeframe for the crypto set. BUIDL lets you stay in the digital world, on the blockchain, earning maybe 3–5% a year, depending on the market, while keeping your money ready to trade or move. It's like a savings account that's open 24/7, backed by BlackRock's rock-solid reputation.

And powering all this innovation is the Solana network. When BUIDL switched to Solana, the SOL token jumped 7% in a week, a clear sign the market was excited. BlackRock chose Solana for good reason. Ethereum, where BUIDL started, is great for smart contracts, but as we've detailed in the book, it is wildly expensive and painfully slow, with fees that can eat into your profits. Solana's lightning-fast transactions and low fees are ideal for a fund like BUIDL, where large sums need to be transferred quickly. If you're trading $1 million in tokens, Ethereum might charge you thousands and make you wait minutes; Solana does it for pennies in a split second. Plus, Solana's DeFi scene is vibrant; you can take your

BUIDL tokens and lend them on various platforms. You can move BUIDL tokens between Solana, Ethereum, or some other protocol, picking up yield along the way. Try doing that with your standard money market fund.

Solana's role is bigger than just BUIDL. While Ethereum holds most tokenized assets, which is still a relatively small asset class, Solana's is gaining share, and BlackRock's move is like a green light for other big players to jump onto the network. What can you do with BUIDL? You can hold the tokens in your wallet to continue earning interest or trade them on Solana's DeFi platforms, such as Raydium or Orca, which are open 24/7. If you want to get creative, use BUIDL tokens as collateral to borrow other assets, like USDC, to fund new trades without selling. A tool called Wormhole lets you move your tokens to other blockchains, so you've got options. But beyond all that, there's a bigger significance to BUIDL.

The arc of the BUIDL story traces the arc of the crypto industry. What started a decade ago as a niche area of fintech eventually grew to be a key component of one of the largest asset managers' crypto plans, a remarkable journey in a relatively short period. In the 2010s, crypto was an area for coders, advanced technologists with a distrust for government and established, and entrenched financial entities. I, like many of my peers, dismissed it without really understanding it, too. But fast-forward a little over a decade later, and it's being openly embraced and integrated into some of the world's largest established financial firms.

What started as a store of value from a white paper of unknown origins has morphed into one of the greatest technological leaps for money since the telegram. Bitcoin opened the door, but now others are breaking through it. Solana launched in 2017, promising speed, but Wall Street stayed skeptical, especially after the 2022 FTX crash. But in the years since the collapse of FTX, what could've been an asset class-destroying event, the financial equivalent of the asteroid killing the dinosaurs proved only to be a major setback. Not only is Bitcoin back, but the entire crypto industry, with people like Fink leading the way, has never been stronger or more vibrant.

Why should you care? Because BUIDL on Solana is a big deal; it brings Wall Street's trust to crypto's speed. For Solana, BlackRock's involvement is like a superstar endorsement, bringing more investors and making the network stronger. For BlackRock, it's a way to show blockchain can handle huge sums, paving the way for more tokenized assets like stocks or real estate. For you, it's a chance to earn steady money in a new system of near-instant trades and instantly available money. After all, it is your money's waiting. It might as well work for you.

Three entirely different companies from three entirely different industries—finance, telecom, and tech—all leveraging the same network to change the world and empower users and investors in various ways. It's the stuff of science fiction, but here's the deal: it's real and happening every day all around the world. It's easy to get distracted by coin prices, and if we're being honest, it occurs to me more than I'd like. A little speculation is healthy and probably beneficial for your portfolio. But as you stare at rising coin prices, don't lose sight of the real bull market, the one in innovation. Solana is at the heart of that, and the world of tomorrow will look nothing like the one I described. I can't wait.

Chapter 10

You Can't à La Carte the Trump Buffet

The morning of January 20, 2025, will go down as one of the strangest of my life. It wasn't just that Donald Trump was about to be sworn back in as the 47th President, clawing his way back to the White House with the unlikeliest of comebacks. That was weird, sure, but it wasn't the weirdest thing. The weirdest thing was that while the TV blared with the red, white, and blue pageantry of Trump's second inauguration, my phone was blowing up with a story that made the inauguration look like a halftime show.

I wasn't scrolling for DC gossip. I'd been down that path before. My 11 days in the White House during Trump's first term were such a short stint that it became a new unit of time: a Scaramucci. I'd seen the man up close, a whirlwind of instinct and impulse, charming one minute, reckless the next. I'd sat through the press conferences, flown on Air Force One, and watched him treat the presidency like a reality show in which he was both starring and producing. So, when he won again, this time with the popular vote, I figured maybe, just maybe, he'd find some peace in victory. Maybe he'd be the "good Trump," the one who could charm a room and actually get things done. Maybe he'd show the promise I always believed existed inside him. Maybe.

But that morning, my phone wasn't buzzing about Trump's return to power. It was about something else entirely: two cryptocurrencies, launched in the dead of night, that had set the financial world on fire while the U.S. stock markets were still asleep. Trump had done so many outrageous things in his first term, berating his hand-picked Fed Chair and tweeting policy changes as if they were Yelp reviews, that most people had lost the capacity to be shocked. But this? This was different. Even the most jaded and jaundiced Trump watchers were staring at their screens, mouths agape, wondering aloud, "Is this legal? How does this even work?"

My attention that morning was split between two screens. One was the TV, which showed Washington, DC, decked out in inaugural splendor, the White House gleaming against the icy air. It was the kind of cold that made you regret taking a breath. A bundled-up Trump and Melania glided through the ceremony, which had been moved indoors for the first time since Reagan because of a deep East Coast freeze. Everything felt sluggish, as if the air itself were molasses.

My other eye was on my phone, which showed a different universe, one that was scorching hot, frenetic, alive. That screen wasn't the live feed of Trump and Melania trudging through DC's arctic chill. It was a static image of them, stylized and electric, tied to a crypto coin that was shooting to the moon. I held my phone up so both screens were in my line of sight: the TV's solemn, frozen pomp split-screened with my phone's manic, retina-searing $TRUMP coin. One was a ritual of power. The other was a casino on steroids. I kept staring at my phone, then back at the TV, trying to make sense of a world where these two realities could coexist. I held up my phone again so that my TV and phone were in the same sightline. On one screen, a man was reclaiming the presidency. On the other, that same man was a Meme, virtual rocket fuel for a financial system that seemed to be rewriting its own rules by the second. If you'd told me a decade ago that the fate of the free world and the crypto markets would be riding on the same guy, I'd have laughed. But that morning, as the cold froze DC and the coins burned up my phone, I wasn't laughing. I was transfixed.

It all started two nights earlier at the Andrew Mellon Auditorium, a large, marble-filled neoclassical building nestled among DC's other imposing fortresses. It would be the stage for the type of spectacle that was straight out of a HODLER's dream. The Mellon Auditorium has seen its share of history, including NATO's birth and Clinton's signing of NAFTA, but that night it was witness to two unsinkable forces: the crypto comeback and Trump's reelection.

The inaugural Crypto Ball was a mashup of two very different cultures, Silicon Valley's techno elite crashing headfirst into MAGA's raw political swagger. The building was lit up like a blockchain, its stone facade crawling with projected data chains straight out of *The Matrix*. Inside, attendees who'd shelled out $100,000 mingled in black-tie, sporting "Make Bitcoin Great Again" hats like they were the new red MAGA caps. It was glitz and grit, a marriage of crypto's wild-eyed optimism and Trump's unapologetic showmanship, and it felt like the future was being born, or at least being loudly announced.

Crypto, once a dirty word in DC, was being openly embarrassed by Trump's pro-Bitcoin agenda. The event, hosted by BTC Inc. and Stand With Crypto, was a victory lap for an industry that had spent years being hounded by the Securities and Exchange Commission and its many detractors on Wall Street. Much like the MAGA movement, Bitcoin could not be destroyed, and there was an unmistakable symbiotic relationship developing between these two entities. They almost seemed to be drawing strength from each other, with each setback overcome, hardening their collective purpose and resolve.

Tickets had sold out weeks ago, and the prices weren't cheap: $2,500 for general admission, $5,000 for "Black" tickets, $100,000 for VIP access to a roped-off perch above the plebs, and $1 million for a package that included a future dinner with the president-elect himself. The dress code was black tie, but the vibe was a mix of Wall Street swagger, tech-bro insouciance, and MAGA bravado. It felt like a bull market on steroids.

The crowd was a colorful mix of crypto elites, political heavyweights, and a few wild cards like Snoop Dogg and Soulja Boy, who later joined Rick Ross for a live performance of his hit single "Crank That." Michael Saylor, the MicroStrategy czar who'd bet his company on Bitcoin, stood out in a tux with a splash of orange, nodding his head to the beat. Brian Armstrong, Coinbase's boyish CEO, mingled with the Winklevoss twins and Peter Thiel, the billionaire venture capitalist who would host an even more exclusive bash the next night at his home. And at the center of it all was man of the moment, David Sacks, Trump's newly minted AI and Crypto Czar, the evening's emcee, and the person Trump tasked with bridging the gap between Washington and Silicon Valley. Sacks almost seemed bemused by the whole thing, almost as if he coded the entire evening into existence, an extension of his own personal Matrix, the culmination of an extraordinary journey that began in the earliest days of digital payments, starting PayPal with Elon Musk and Peter Thiel before selling it to eBay for billions.

His eyes don't just see the room; they saw through and everyone in it. After all, it was his reality that they were living in, forged through sheer force of will. Who else could bring together Snoop Dogg and Brian Armstrong? The pounding bass and lyrics from Soulja Boy ricocheted through the hallowed halls.

"Soulja Boy off in it oh. Watch me crank it. Watch me roll. Watch me crank that Soulja Boy."

The music shook everything in the room, but Sacks remained still as stone, a chiseled smile of pearly whites framed against a black tuxedo. He spoke to his guests in the same smooth, cool tone that's now so familiar to many, thanks to his smash hit *All In Podcast*. He was all poise and polish, and the Crypto Ball was just another example of him betting right. He was right about PayPal. He was right about Yammer and SpaceX. And of course, he was right about crypto. And now, he was right about the election, having been an early and vociferous Trump supporter.

President Trump, of course, hadn't always been the biggest Bitcoin backer. At various times during his first term, he called Bitcoin a "scam" and dismissed cryptocurrencies as tools for drug dealers and tax evaders. But by 2024, things started to change, helped along by some unforced errors in the Democratic Party. Crypto had moved mainstream, fueled by Reddit threads and TikTok influencers; CNBC even put it on regular rotation on its ticker, alongside the DOW, gold, and the 10-year bond. Trump, sensing an opportunity, jumped on board with typical abandon. During his campaign, he accepted Bitcoin donations, floated the idea of a national Bitcoin reserve, and promised to make the United States the "crypto capital of the planet." His sons, Eric and Donald Jr., had already dipped their toes in the water with World Liberty Financial, a crypto venture. The stars were aligning, and two bets that seemed like long shots just years ago, the return of Trump and record Bitcoin prices, were converging with astonishing speed.

The crypto industry, finally sensing a potential friend in Washington in the second Trump administration, poured millions into his campaign and inaugural festivities, culminating in the over-the-top night. For crypto enthusiasts, the inauguration wasn't just a political event; it was the dawn of a new era. Finally, a forward thinking pro-crypto administration manned by the very people who built the industry and knew exactly what it needed.

The political contingent was equally impressive, if slightly less eclectic. House Speaker Mike Johnson chatted with Senator Cynthia Lummis, the visionary Wyoming Senator who saw before anyone else in Congress the importance of the crypto economy. Future Treasury Secretary Scott Bessent, a hedge fund titan who learned at the knee of George Soros, surveyed the scene with characteristic calm. No dancing out to Snoop Dogg for him. Everyone who was anyone was in that room. And the incongruity didn't stop with rappers and politicians. Even the food and beverage choice, in a not-so-subtle homage to Trump, was a study in opposites and opulence. McDonald's Quarter Pounders shared equal space on silver platters with lobster rolls and caviar.

Sacks, the man of the moment, was about to address the crowd and throw them into an even bigger tizzy than Soulja Boy. Sacks is as refined and cool as they come, but his polished patina masks a fierce competitor. They don't call it the PayPal mafia for nothing. He can be loyal, funny, biting, and ruthless, all perfect qualities for a crypto kingmaker. He's old school, but he still represents the new guard, a dizzying mix of ambition, brains, and brass.

He slowly glided to the center of the room, perfectly hitting his mark between two 60-foot Doric marble columns. An assistant with astonishing efficiency handed him a mic and just as quickly slipped away like a ghost. A deep red light splashed onto the stage, illuminating Sacks and creating a Darth Vader–like effect against his black tuxedo.

"Ladies and gentlemen," Sacks said in his baritone voice. "Ladies and gentlemen. The reign of terror against crypto is over." Thunderous applause. "And the beginning of innovation in America for crypto has just begun."

More applause!

Sacks argued that crypto was critical to maintaining the United States' financial dominance. The Trump administration, under his direction, would make America the "crypto capital of the world," Sacks told the crowd to more applause. His speech didn't lay out any specific policy objectives, but it set an optimistic tone about the future of the crypto industry. It was all the crowd needed to hear.

If ever anyone could see into the future, it was Sacks. He was right about everything. Whatever you think of Trump, unlike Biden, Trump surrounded himself with people who understood and were supportive of crypto. They intuitively grasped how and why crypto represented the next frontier in financial innovation. Why shouldn't the United States lead the world in this crucial category? Why would you appoint a Czarist SEC Chairman like Gary Gensler to choke and destroy a vibrant industry? It made no sense, regardless of one's political affiliation.

For the attendees, the speech was like mainlining heroin. Politicians, MAGA hat–wearing investors, crypto bros, technologists, and everyone else in attendance roared at every opportunity. The future was about to be coded, and these guys had the keys. It was a masterclass in comebacks, and at times, it was also hard to even process. Was this real? Or some type of vodka-induced tokenized fantasy? If you told me three years ago that David Sacks would be Trump's crypto Czar and that Mike Johnson and Snoop Dogg would be huddled in deep conversation while servers whisked around them with silver platters of fast food and fish roe, all in celebration of the second Trump administration, I'd say you were smoking crack. But here they all were, moving and grooving to the soulful sounds of Snoop Dogg & Co., a scene that was equal parts Great Gatsby and a DevCon gathering. HODLers with glasses of Dom Perignon toasting politicians who just learned what a blockchain was. Billionaire investors and entrepreneurs dancing with Rick Ross in a speculative orgy of fame, wealth, and ambition.

And then things got really weird.

At 9 p.m., the soon-to-be President Trump, who wasn't even at the event, took to Truth Social, his social media platform whose stock behaved like a Meme coin, and in characteristic all-caps pounded out a simple message, soon echoed on X, the very same platform that banned him four years earlier, that sent the building into bedlam.

"My NEW Official Trump MEME is HERE! It's time to celebrate everything we stand for: WINNING! Join my very special Trump Community. GET YOUR $TRUMP NOW. Go to gettrumpMEMEs.com—Have Fun!" The site was careful to point out that buying $TRUMP was an "expression of support" for the president-elect, not an investment, but the real message was clear: this was a chance to ride the Trump train to the moon.

The news exploded.

Audible gasps filled the grand room as stunned traders, many of whom were already half-drunk on crypto-themed cocktails, furiously checked their phones in a desperate attempt to get in. If Soulja Boy dancing with Mike Johnson was hard to process, then this was downright unbelievable. Through various social media platforms, the future and former President announced the launch of $TRUMP, a Solana-based Meme coin complete with an image of Trump raising a defiant fist that appeared to be pulled from his July assassination attempt. X, formerly known as Twitter, and of course, owned by Trump backer and crypto enthusiast Elon Musk, was vibrating. Some speculated Trump's account had been hacked and that the whole thing was a scam. It didn't matter; they were buying no matter what, because this thing was going higher.

Five hundred miles north, in his Upper East Side New York apartment, Anthony Pompliano, or Pomp as he is known, just stared at his phone, as if it were a portal to some alternate universe, one where the incoming president leverages his brand to drop a coin two days before returning to office. The sheer audacity of it gripped him: a former president, a political lightning rod, slapping his name on a digital token like a raw piece of meat and casually tossing it into the crypto lion's den. It was a move so brazen it didn't seem reel.

Pomp's mind went to the incentives. He got why Trump did it. The man's been branding everything from steaks to skyscrapers for decades, turning his name into a kind of currency long before anyone minted a coin in his likeness. This wasn't a leap; it was a natural extension, a digital collectible for a digital age. But Pomp knew the pushback would come, questions about legitimacy, about whether this was a stunt or a scam. And yet, he saw something deeper, something that fit into a framework that he'd been mulling over for years: the reputational premium.

In Pomp's world, every asset has a story, and every story has a price. He mapped it out in his mind: on one end, you've got Berkshire Hathaway, a rock-solid company that's 95% fundamentals and 5% Warren Buffett's aura, what he and other investors called the "Buffett premium." When Buffett's health wobbles, the stock dips, not because the company's weaker but because the man's myth carries weight. Then there's Tesla, a 50-50 split between its electric car empire and Elon Musk's Meme-fueled charisma. DJT, Trump's media stock? That's 5% business, 95% Trump's larger-than-life brand. And the $TRUMP coin? 100% Trump, Pomp thought, leaning into the idea with the glee of someone who's just cracked a code. It's not about cash flows or balance sheets; it's about belief, about the cult of personality distilled into a token you can buy on a blockchain.

This wasn't just a crypto stunt to Pomp; it was a data point, a market signal. Would it work? That was the question buzzing through his head as he scrolled X, watching the reactions pour in. And when it did work, when the coins surged and the Crypto Ball became a cultural flashpoint, Pomp saw confirmation of what he'd long suspected: people don't just invest in fundamentals anymore. They invest in stories, in brands, in the gravitational pull of a name. Trump, love him or hate him, had that pull, and he'd just monetized it in a way no politician had before.

Pomp is no stranger to the wild swings of markets, crypto or otherwise. A former Army sergeant who traded his combat boots for a suit and a stint at Morgan Stanley, Pomp has carved out a reputation as one of crypto's loudest evangelists. After cutting his teeth in venture capital and founding Pomp Investments, he became a fixture on CNBC and his own podcast, *The Pomp Podcast*, where he breaks down markets in a simple and approachable style that appeals to investors of all stripes. He's a guy who's seen bubbles inflate and pop, from dot-com to DeFi, and he's got a knack for spotting inflection points. So when the $TRUMP coin news broke, he didn't just gawk; he dissected it.

The irony wasn't lost on Pomp. Trump, a guy who'd once called crypto a scam, was now launching a Meme coin with his face on it.

It was the kind of plot twist that could make you laugh or wince. To Pomp, it wasn't hypocrisy; it was pragmatism. Trump understood collectibles, just as he understood how to sell a building or a TV show. Crypto was just another canvas for his brand, and now the technology could support it. What were the future implications? Could monetizing brands be the next great asset class? Who knows, but the market was speaking loudly. The Crypto Ball, with its glitz and its Memes, wasn't an outlier; it was a mirror held up to a world where reputation is as tradable as gold.

As the Crypto Ball faded into the rearview, Pomp kept his eyes on the bigger picture. The $TRUMP coin wasn't about just crypto's fundamentals or even Solana's technology; it was about the power of a name to move markets. It was a reminder that in this game, perception often trumps reality (pun intended), and the crowd will pay a premium for a story they believe in. For Pomp, who had built his career on spotting those stories early, it was validation that his reputational bet on crypto was not only spot on but also had one hell of a future.

Within moments, the coin's market cap had hit $1 billion. The crypto world didn't know what to make of it at first. Some were unsure if the whole thing was a joke or some type of elaborate scam or if his social account had been hacked. But as more and more posts on X appeared, the skepticism gave way to a classic crypto emotion, fear of missing out, or FOMO. $TRUMP, priced at 18 cents at launch, began to surge. Within minutes, $TRUMP passed $1.00, then $2.00, then $3.00. Each passing milestone was met with increasing incredulity. It was just the start of a surreal journey that by midnight would see the coin touch $6.50. By 3 a.m. it hit a mind-blowing $33.87, a staggering 18,000% gain in hours. And there was tons of liquidity. Trading volume exploded, with billions of dollars changing hands. The coin's market cap soared to $5 billion, then $7.6 billion, vaulting it into the top 30 cryptocurrencies globally. The frenzy was so intense that traders actually started selling other, more popular and established coins just to buy $TRUMP.

Pomp could hold back any longer. He joined the fray on X from his apartment.

"The incoming President of the United States just launched a Meme coin days before his inauguration," Pomp posted. *"Financial markets are not ready for what is ahead. Buckle up."*

Back in DC, no one was wearing a seatbelt.

The hall, bathed in deep red lights, began to take on a shade of purple from the blue light emanating from people opening their phones. It was an instant, if not unconventional, affirmation for the true believers and HODLers. The industry, in a very short period, had gone from Bitcoin being a $0.01 in 2009 to the President of the United States launching an on-chain Meme coin on a rival blockchain. The naysayers had nothing left to say. For better or worse, the leader of the free world had just dropped the crypto mic.

It was time for a little Snoop Dogg.

"Drop it like it's hahhht. Drop it like it's hahhht," Snoop crooned.

Heads bobbing. Memes surging. Booze flowing. Soulja Boy, who'd once shilled his own dubious coins, danced as if he had just bought a bag of $TRUMP. But beneath the glitz, something deeper was happening. The Crypto Ball was confirmation that the industry had gone from pariah to power player. Trump, once a Bitcoin skeptic, had completely reversed and unabashedly embraced the most speculative aspects of the asset class. And, it was payback of sorts. His campaign had raised millions from crypto donors, and his inaugural committee had shattered records with hundreds of millions in contributions, much of it from digital asset firms.

For many of the so-called true believers, the night was a glimpse of a future they'd been building in exile. Clumsy, ill-conceived, and poorly administered regulations had driven much of the crypto world and innovation offshore. Many of the most interesting projects were now being built in Asia and tropical islands. Trump's rules could change that, or so the collective thinking went.

And what better way to show support for the industry than to speak their language and drop an on-chain Meme coin, two days before his inauguration? It was a simultaneous hug of this new, loyal community and a fully extended middle finger to Biden and his hapless SEC Chair Gensler. As the kids might say, the future was gonna be lit. The importance of the moment could not be understated, and for a couple hours, the activities in the Mellon Auditorium served as a metaphor for a brave new world, a world where crypto bros, politicians, rappers, and billionaire investors all congregated to celebrate a president who'd turned their niche obsession into a national reserve. The Crypto Ball was more than a celebration of Trump. It was a coronation of the crypto cognoscenti that blurred the lines of politics, celebrity, finance, and technology. So many in that same room had spent the last decade excluded from other people's parties. Now, they were the party, and the world's attention only seemed to expand their already swollen egos and pride.

Chapter 11

The Meme King Reacts

Joe McCann was playing with his kids when the world tried to pull him back into the circus. He was holed up in his Portland, Oregon, house, a second home away from his usual Miami haunt, surrounded by the cheerful chaos of his four-year-old son and two-year-old daughter. The living room looked like a battlefield of LEGOs, stuffed animals, and half-eaten Goldfish crackers. His daughter, who'd just turned two on Christmas Day, was gleefully smacking a toy piano, while his son staged an elaborate saga involving a dinosaur and a dump truck. McCann was fully present, down on the carpet, assembling one of the many Christmas gifts. This was his sanctuary, the one place where the relentless ping of his phone couldn't intrude.

Except tonight, it did.

The phone buzzed once, twice, then a third time, each vibration like a pebble in a still pond. McCann ignored it at first, but the buzzing became insistent, a digital tantrum. He glanced at the screen and saw a text from his PR agent, Lisa, a woman whose enthusiasm for his brand sometimes outstripped his own. "Joe, this is it!" the message read. "The victory lap of all victory laps! Trump just launched a Meme coin on Solana! *Every* journalist wants you!" McCann chuckled. He typed back, "With my kids. Not now," and tossed the phone onto the couch. But the news was too big to ignore, even for a guy who'd built a career surfing the wildest waves of the Internet. Donald Trump, the newly re-elected president, had just announced the $TRUMP coin on Truth Social at 9 p.m., right in the middle of a decadent Crypto Ball tied to his inauguration. And McCann, the Meme King, was supposed to have an opinion.

A torrent of Meme memories hit McCann, his 2023 bet on BONK, Shiba Inu, and Dogwifhat, all earning him the title of Meme King, a title that both flattered and annoyed him, pigeonholing him as the guy who made millions betting on fart coins and dog pics while the suits at Goldman Sachs tsk-tsked. But McCann didn't care about the suits. He cared about the invisible currents of culture that could turn a silly logo into a fortune. And the $TRUMP coin? That was a pattern he couldn't ignore, even if it intruded on his alone time with his kids.

When his kids finally went to sleep and the toys were abandoned, McCann picked up his phone. He wasn't about to call Lisa back; she'd have him on the phone with CNBC before he could blink, but he was curious. He opened TradingView, his go-to app for tracking markets, a kind of Bloomberg for people who didn't wear ties. TradingView didn't list most Meme coins, but there it was: the $TRUMP coin launched on Solana with a logo that was pure MAGA kitsch, a golden caricature of Trump's face, hair swooped like a soft-serve cone, set against a red, white, and blue background. Not quite a dog, but pretty darn good. The price was already spiking, up 200% since the Truth Social post. McCann leaned back on the couch, his mind racing. He wasn't shocked. Trump was a kind of Meme incarnate, a walking, talking Internet phenomenon who'd turned outrage and audacity into a brand. A $TRUMP coin made sense, especially on Solana. BONK had thrived on Solana's speed and scalability, and McCann had long argued that Solana was the future of tokenization. The $TRUMP coin was a test case, a brash, in-your-face experiment that could either crash spectacularly or redefine the game.

McCann's reaction wasn't glee or skepticism; it was a kind of weary recognition. He'd seen this movie before. The coin had all the ingredients: a viral figurehead, a polarizing logo, and Solana's technical edge. But it also had baggage. Trump was divisive, a lightning rod who had galvanized half the country and alienated the other half. Meme coins thrived on universal appeal. Dogs were safe, lovable, and a shortcut to the heart. Trump was a gamble, a coin that could soar on MAGA fervor but crash if the broader market recoiled. McCann switched over to Telegram chats, where the vibe was a mix.

There were tons of "TO THE MOON!" posts, but an equal amount of snarky ones, too. "This is dumber than Fart Coin!" exclaimed one. He didn't post. He never did. He just watched, his mind cataloging the chatter, the sentiment, the patterns. What struck him most was the timing. The coin had dropped two days before Trump's inauguration, during the Crypto Ball that was sure to grab universal attention. It was a ballsy move, but it was also the kind of stunt that screamed Trump. McCann imagined the scene exactly as it was: crypto bros in tuxedos, influencers snapping selfies, and a giant screen flashing the $TRUMP logo while a DJ spun Savage. It was the kind of spectacle that could launch a coin into orbit or bury it under its own hype. McCann's gut told him it would be the former, at least for a while. The coin was already trending on X, with posts racking up thousands of likes. He checked AssetDash again: $TRUMP's market cap was pushing $1 billion. Not bad for a few hours.

He thought back to his BONK bet, the one that had made him the Meme King. BONK had been a no-brainer: a dog, a clean narrative, and Solana's tech. The $TRUMP coin was messier, more like a political campaign than a Meme coin. But it had potential. Solana's low fees and high performance enabled it to handle the trading frenzy, unlike Ethereum, where gas fees and congestion would have ruined any chance of success.

And tokenization, this idea that anything could be turned into a tradable asset, was Solana's superpower. BlackRock's Larry Fink had been banging that drum, talking about tokenizing stocks and bonds. McCann had been saying the same thing, just with dogs instead of equities. Meme coins were the first major test of tokenization, a proof of concept that demonstrated the ability to assign a billion-dollar valuation to something as intangible as a Meme. The $TRUMP coin was the next step, a test of whether a person, a brand as big as Trump, could be tokenized in the same way.

McCann didn't buy it that night. He wasn't impulsive, despite what a moniker like Meme King might suggest. He'd watch, wait, and let the market show its hand. His kids were his priority, and the markets would still be there in the morning. But as he walked past their bedrooms, he couldn't help but smile. The Meme King had called it years ago: Solana was the future, and Meme coins were its vanguard. The $TRUMP coin, for all its noise and baggage, was just another chapter in the story he'd been writing since BONK. The world was catching up, and Joe McCann, with his apps, his instincts, and his unshakable faith in the absurd, was already ahead of the curve.

Thousands of miles away, Crypto Ball was ending. But the party was just starting.

Chapter 12

Melania Meme

The world and crypto universe in particular were still in a state of shock, like a boxer who had been hit with a devastating jab, stumbling to make sense of events when the knockout punch arrived in the form of another post on X. The $TRUMP coin was still surging, now worth more than Ford, leaving mouths agape when another shocker ripped through the crypto universe, leaving traders in an even greater sense of confusion. Just over 48 hours after her husband shocked the world with the launch of the $TRUMP coin, and less than 24 hours before she was about to return to the White House, the incoming First Lady dropped her own crypto bombshell.

On January 19, 2025, at 5:30 p.m. EST, she posted on X to her 3.2 million followers:

"The Official Melania MEME is live! You can buy $MELANIA now."

Unlike her husband's coin, which evoked his horrible assassination attempt, Melania's branding was decidedly softer. It was written in elegant fonts and featured a black-and-white photo of her smiling, hands clasped as if in gratitude. It looked like a mashup of Vogue and CoinDesk, but while the imagery was different, the intent was the same: cash in on the Trump mystique. Distributed by MKT World LLC, her Florida-based company, $MELANIA was pegged as a "digital collectible" to support her initiatives, and much like her husband's coin, it was careful to point out that it was an "expression of support for and engagement with the values embodied by the symbol MELANIA" and not in any way an "investment opportunity, investment contract, or security of any type."

Investors apparently weren't reading the fine print. By Monday morning, it was trading at $11.22, with a $2.15 billion valuation, and had cracked the top 60 cryptocurrencies, according to *Forbes*. Within less than 24 hours, it had increased in value by 256%.

But the timing was no accident. Melania's launch came just as $TRUMP was peaking, and some traders, sensing a new shiny object, sold their $TRUMP to pile into $MELANIA, causing a brief dip in the former. The crypto markets, already dizzy from $TRUMP's ascent, reeled. Melania's launch triggered a 40% crash in $TRUMP's value, wiping out $5 billion in market cap as traders sold off one $TRUMP coin to chase the other. It was as if the first couple had turned the blockchain into a family affair, each coin vying for supremacy in a zero-sum game. The Trumps, poised to deregulate crypto, were now its most volatile players.

The volatility was breathtaking. $MELANIA hit $13.73 by Monday afternoon and then plummeted below $4 by evening, stabilizing at $3–$4 on January 21, per Capital.com. $TRUMP, meanwhile, clawed back to $60. The cryptocurrency world, accustomed to wild swings, was nonetheless gob smacked. If there were any questions about Trump's commitment to crypto, the midnight madness of the Meme coins put that to rest. The $TRUMP and $MELANIA coins, launched on the eve of his inauguration, were a signal: the Trumps weren't just endorsing cryptocurrency; they were going to drive it. It was a collision of worlds, politics, finance, tech, and celebrity, moving at the speed of a Meme on X. Crypto had always been its own brand of finance, replete with technicolor characters, but now the ringmaster was the President of the United

States, and the tent was packed with speculators, true believers, and, now, the First Lady, all vying for attention. $MELANIA coin, with its glossy website and vague promises of "empowering freedom," was more a cultural artifact than a financial instrument.

Across the country, the crypto faithful were watching, some with glee, others with dread. The coin's launch was a gauntlet thrown at the feet of an industry that prided itself on decentralization, on being the antidote to centralized power and political pageantry. For every trader pumping the coin on X, there was a developer wincing at the thought of crypto becoming a prop in Trump's show. The irony was thick: a technology born to bypass gatekeepers was now being co-opted by the ultimate gatekeeper, a man whose brand would be added to a cryptocurrency, alongside a collection of skyscrapers, golf courses, and steaks. And yet, the market didn't care about irony. Prices spiked, wallets opened, and the blockchain churned.

I always said you can't à la carte Trump. You get the full buffet, whether you want it or not. You're not just going to get the fruit. You're going to get fruit, omelets, bagels, pastries, cereal, bacon, pancakes, and overcooked Eggs Benedict. There was no picking or choosing. You had to take all of him in. The forward-thinking approach to crypto? Loved it. Surrounding himself with people who built and understood this nascent industry? Loved it even more. Launching a Meme coin the night before the inauguration. Not a fan. But I knew crypto was stronger than a presidential stunt, no matter how big.

After all, this wasn't the first time crypto had been swept up in a cultural storm. Bitcoin had survived Mt. Gox, Silk Road, and a thousand scams, to say nothing of FTX's collapse. Ethereum had weathered its own dramas. But $TRUMP and $MELANIA felt different, less like a bubble and more like a realization, forcing the industry to confront its own contradictions. Was crypto still the rebel outpost of coders and cypherpunks, or had it become just another stage for the loudest voices with the biggest megaphones? The question hung in the air, unanswered, as the coin's market cap climbed into the billions, fueled by a mix of MAGA loyalists, day traders, and bots amplifying the noise.

Meanwhile, in the quieter corners of the Internet, the old guard was wrestling with the spectacle. These were the people who'd built the pipes, the blockchains, the protocols. They weren't in it for the headlines or the Lambos; they were in it for the math, for the elegant logic of distributed systems. To them, $MELANIA was a sideshow. A dangerous one. It wasn't just the risk of a pump-and-dump or a regulatory crackdown; it was the way it distorted the signal, turning a revolution into a reality show. They'd seen this before, celebrity coins, Meme tokens, hype cycles that left retail investors holding the bag, but this time, the stakes felt higher, the audience bigger, the fallout potentially catastrophic.

And so, as the X posts piled up and the price charts MOONED, a quiet tension spread through the crypto world. It was the tension between the dream of a decentralized future and the reality of a market driven by human nature, greed, fear, and endless hunger for attention. That tension was about to find a voice, not in a board-room or a trading floor, but in an apartment on the edge of San Francisco, where the creator of Solana took stock of the madness.

Chapter 13

Only in America

Three thousand miles away, Anatoly Yakovenko was sprawled on his couch in his San Francisco apartment. The room was dimly lit, a laptop glowing on the coffee table, casting shadows across a clutter of glasses and books. Yakovenko was in a rare moment of calm. No meetings, no bug reports, just the soft buzz of his phone and the faint sound of the world outside. He was scrolling X, half-distracted, when the calm was shattered.

A post caught his eye. A retweet, then another, then a torrent of them, like dominoes toppling in real time. "Trump just launched a Meme coin on Solana," one read, followed by a screenshot of a tweet from the incoming president's account. Yakovenko froze, his thumb hovering over the screen. His first thought wasn't triumph or pride but raw, instinctive panic. "Oh my God, his account has been hacked," he muttered, sitting up so fast the couch creaked. His mind raced to worst-case scenarios. Was it a security breach, a prank, or worse? This wasn't just any coin. It was a presidential stunt, a digital Molotov cocktail lobbed into the crypto markets.

Yakovenko's X timeline was a firehose. Posts piled up, some gleeful, others skeptical, all amplifying the same bombshell. $TRUMP was blazing a trail across the Solana superhighway. Posts about "Making Crypto Great Again" tore through his feed. Yakovenko clicked through to Trump's account, half-expecting a disclaimer indicating the account was hacked. No such luck. The tweet was real, pinned at the top, racking up thousands of retweets by the minute. His phone buzzed with notifications from friends, colleagues, random crypto investors, all tagging him with "@anatolyyak, you seeing this??"

He wasn't seeing it so much as feeling it, a visceral jolt like the moment before a big wave crashes. Yakovenko's first move was to fire a message off to Gokal. "Is this real?" he typed, his heart thumping. Then he pinged Phil Chang, their chief legal counsel, the guy who knew how to navigate the murky waters of crypto regulation. "Guys, what's going on? Is Trump's account compromised?" The replies came quickly, cautiously, and non-committally. "Seems. . .real," Gokal said. Chang echoed the sentiment: "No confirmation it's fake, but we're checking." Yakovenko stared at his screen; the retweets were piling up, Crypto Twitter was losing its collective minds. But while all this was happening, the Solana network was humming along just fine. They had never seen volume like this, but the fees stayed muted. Everything appeared to be working. For now.

Yakovenko waited, staring at his laptop, where a dashboard showed Solana's network metrics. Fees. Network rates. So far, nothing unusual, but the tweet was only minutes old. If this were real, a way bigger deluge was coming, and it would be a torrent of traders, speculators, and bots piling in to ride the Trump train. Solana had handled NFT frenzies and DeFi surges, but this was different. This was a cultural earthquake, a moment where the world's eyes would be on his creation, judging whether it could deliver or crumble.

Amid the chaos and fear, Yakovenko's mind drifted back to 2021, when Solana's network had buckled under the weight of the NFT boom. Degenerate Apes and other projects had drawn bot armies spamming transactions, overwhelming the Solana network and causing it to crash for almost a day. That experience was a baptism by fire, a useful lesson that only made the network stronger. The network's crash was a stake to the heart, but they made the proper fixes and moved on. But this was different. The Degenerate Apes were important to the Solana community, but they were relatively unknown to noncrypto enthusiasts. Sure, the network outage was a black eye and an embarrassment, but it wasn't a global catastrophe. If there were a failure caused by $TRUMP, it would be lights out for Solana. They'd be finished, unable to recover from the presidential Meme coin mass hysteria. $TRUMP was bigger than any NFT drop. Could the network handle it?

If we crash now, Yakovenko thought, it's over. The crypto world was unforgiving, quick to crown but even quicker to kill. Ethereum, slower but battle-tested, loomed as the safe bet. If Solana faltered, the narrative would write itself: "Trump coin breaks Solana! Ethereum is still king." He could already hear the X posts, the smug "I told you so" from Ethereum fans. Moreover, a crash would undermine Solana's core thesis that it can sync markets and payments at breakneck speed without congestion. "If we crash, people would say Ethereum's safer," Yakovenko told Gokal.

For the next 48 hours, Yakovenko and his team at Solana Labs adopted a policy of radio silence. No tweets, no statements, no engagement with the $TRUMP coin frenzy. "Engage with a coin" is crypto-speak for promoting it, hyping it, or even acknowledging its existence in a way that might be construed as an endorsement. And Yakovenko wasn't about to touch this one with a 10-foot pole. Not until they knew it was real. Not until they were sure the network could handle the load. Because if Solana buckled under the weight of a presidential Meme coin, it wouldn't just be a bad day. It would be an existential crisis for a project that had bet everything on being the world's fastest and most scalable blockchain. Since that fateful blackout, Yakovenko and his team had spent years hardening the system, optimizing the code, and stress-testing every component. By 2025, Solana had become a powerhouse, handling massive token launches with ease. But nothing, absolutely nothing, could prepare them for the $TRUMP coin.

Within hours, the $TRUMP coin was generating 10% of the Nasdaq's average daily trading volume, nearly $40 billion in transactions according to internal figures, a number that made Yakovenko's head spin. Bots were flooding the network, arbitrageurs were pouncing, and retail traders were FOMOing with their life savings. The fees were rising, sure, but they weren't spiking into the stratosphere like Ethereum's had. "It's holding," Yakovenko whispered to himself, almost afraid to jinx it.

Then came the hiccup. Tether, one of Solana's biggest stablecoin providers, had a glitch. Their servers, overwhelmed by the $TRUMP coin frenzy, briefly went offline. Fees on some Solana markets spiked, not catastrophically, but enough to make Yakovenko wince. It was a reminder of how fragile even the best systems could be. "If you don't implement this right," he told Gokal later, "we end up like Ethereum. Slow, expensive, congested." But the network didn't crash. The validators, thousands of computers around the world keeping Solana running, kept humming. The fees stabilized. The system worked.

For Yakovenko, it was more than a technical win. It was a validation of Solana's entire thesis. The dream was to build a blockchain where high-stakes markets, even the unlikely scenario of a presidential Meme coin, could coexist with everyday transactions, like paying for coffee with USDC. If fees spiked every time a hot token launched, companies like PayPal would ditch Solana and build their own networks. "They'd spin up their own L1," Yakovenko warned colleagues, using crypto jargon for a L1 blockchain. "They don't want their users getting hit with congestion." The $TRUMP coin launch was the ultimate stress test, an impromptu, high-stakes, global pop quiz that proved Solana could handle both Wall Street and Main Street without breaking a sweat.

Yakovenko smiled and looked out his window. He could see his neighborhood, but in his mind, he saw the America that took him in as a kid, the one that educated him, nurtured his dreams, and gave him the very tools to make those dreams come true. He thought back to all the hard work at the University of Illinois, the long hours in the lab, the scribbling on the napkin at Cafe Solie that would later become the idea for Solana. A kid from Ukraine, arriving with just $50 in his pocket, would go on to build a network that would rewire global finance, catch the eye of a president known for his reality-TV flair, and create billions in value. He thought back to high school, where he wrote programs for fun and hacked together games and tools on a secondhand PC. Yakovenko's story is the American Dream in binary. Solana's success, capped by a presidential coin, felt surreal. Wow, he thought to himself. This couldn't happen anywhere else.

Chapter 14

The Future

Rare, generational trades mark the history of wealth creation, opportunities so profound that they redefine lives and reshape economies. Bitcoin's meteoric rise from less than a dollar to over $100,000 and counting stands as one of the greatest trades ever, a testament to the power of early adoption in transformative technologies. I was lucky to get in late, but early enough to change my firm's fortunes. Similarly, companies like Apple, Nvidia, and Microsoft have delivered life-changing returns for those who recognized their potential early. Now, Solana is emerging as the next generational trade, a platform poised to redefine economies, empower individuals, and birth a new era of innovation. I got into this trade early, and I intend to stay with it for as long as possible.

Solana is not just a blockchain; it's a catalyst for new economies. Its technology has made it a playground for the unimaginable, transforming complex ideas into intuitive, accessible realities. Solana is digitizing the physical world, transforming objects into virtual assets that can be traded, owned, and monetized in ways previously unimaginable. From real estate to collectibles, physical and digital boundaries are dissolving, creating a fluid marketplace where anything can become an asset.

This transformation extends beyond objects. Solana enables individuals to commoditize their reputation, image, or personal brand, unlocking new avenues for economic participation. Imagine a world where creators, influencers, or even everyday people can tokenize their personal value, whether it's their expertise, social capital, or creative output, and trade it on a global stage, just like a stock. This is not science fiction; it's happening now. We're seeing companies leverage Solana to revolutionize money management, with decentralized finance platforms offering unprecedented access to financial tools. Entire networks, from phone services to mapping systems, are springing up on the Solana blockchain, redefining how we connect, navigate, and interact. Who knows what's next? In a world where innovation knows no bounds, Solana is the foundation for what's possible.

The implications are staggering, especially for younger generations who live their lives through their phones. For them, the virtual world is as real as the physical one. There are no lines between the two. Social media, gaming, and digital communities dominate their daily experiences, blurring the lines between what is "real" and what is virtual. If the virtual world has no limits, imagine what that means for the global economy. Solana's ability to create frictionless, scalable, and decentralized systems positions it as the backbone of this virtual economy, where ideas, assets, and opportunities flow freely. This is not just about trading tokens or building businesses; it's about empowering individuals to participate in a global marketplace like never before.

Consider the billions of people living in underserved regions or struggling economies. Many lack access to quality education, capital, or traditional business infrastructure, yet they possess brilliant ideas and untapped potential. Historically, these individuals have been locked out of global markets, their genius stifled by circumstance. Solana changes that. By providing a decentralized platform accessible to anyone with an Internet connection, Solana equips these potential visionaries with the tools to turn ideas into reality. A farmer in a remote village can tokenize their land's output, a coder in a developing nation can build a decentralized app, and a creator anywhere can monetize their work, all free from intermediaries or gatekeepers. This democratization of opportunity is Solana's true promise: a world where great ideas, not just great resources, drive success.

This potential is amplified by the convergence of Solana with artificial intelligence, a partnership that could redefine the global economy. AI is already reshaping industries, from healthcare to logistics, but its full potential remains untapped. When paired with Solana's blockchain, AI can power decentralized applications that are faster, smarter, and more accessible than ever. Imagine AI-driven financial advisors operating on Solana, offering personalized wealth strategies to anyone with a smartphone. Picture AI-enhanced marketplaces where creators and consumers trade value in real time, secured on the Solana blockchain. This marriage of blockchain and AI could spark a golden age, an era where human creativity and computational power unite to solve problems, create wealth, and redefine productivity.

It could be the new golden age, one that surpasses the Industrial Revolution, which mechanized labor, or the Information Age, which connected the world through data. We may be on the cusp of a Virtual Revolution, where blockchains like Solana serve as protocols for productivity, enabling seamless collaboration between humans and machines. In this future, Solana is not just a platform for transactions; it's a foundation for innovation, where ideas are the currency and blockchains are the infrastructure. This revolution will empower individuals, dismantle barriers, and create opportunities on an unprecedented scale.

I was fortunate to receive advice from Michael Saylor, who's better than anyone at spotting and capitalizing on transformative technologies. He told me, "If you see a generational trade, don't stop. Buy it, buy it again, buy more, and then tweet about it." His words resonate deeply with Solana's potential. Just as Amazon birthed a new economy of e-commerce and Apple's iPhone and app ecosystem created a digital revolution, Solana is poised to build a new economic paradigm. It's a platform where developers, creators, and entrepreneurs can craft solutions that redefine industries, spanning finance, communication, and entertainment. The Solana ecosystem is a dynamic, living network of innovation, and its impact is only just beginning to unfold.

This is why Solana must be part of your portfolio. Whether you invest in the SOL coin itself, explore applications built on the network, or participate in its growing ecosystem, Solana offers an entry point into a world that's becoming real before our eyes. It's not just about financial returns. It's about aligning yourself with a technology that's reshaping how value is created, shared, and experienced. Solana is the gateway to an almost imaginary world, one where the boundaries of possibility are limited only by our imagination.

The excitement surrounding Solana is palpable. Developers are flocking to the platform. Entrepreneurs are building businesses that challenge traditional models, from decentralized social networks to tokenized real-world assets. Communities are forming around shared visions of a decentralized future, where power is distributed and opportunities are universal. This is not a fleeting trend; it's a paradigm shift. Solana is enabling a world where anyone, anywhere, can participate in the global economy, provided they have an idea and an Internet connection.

As we stand on the brink of this transformation, the question is not whether Solana will succeed but by how much? Will it redefine entire industries? Will it empower billions to rise above their circumstances? Will it, alongside AI, spark a revolution that historians will study for centuries to come? I believe the answer to all these questions is a resounding yes. The future is coming faster than we think, and Solana is leading the charge.

So, take Michael Saylor's advice: don't just dip your toes in. Dive in. Invest in Solana, explore its ecosystem, and share the vision. This is more than a trade. It's a chance to be part of a new economy, a new world, and a new era of human potential.

I'm beyond excited. Are you?

Acknowledgments

This book explores how the future of money is rapidly merging with its present and how Solana, a fast and brilliant network, is bringing to life technologies and possibilities once thought unimaginable. However, no future can exist without a past, and I am particularly fortunate to have a past that includes a network of colleagues, friends, and family who have made my once unthinkable future a reality.

I want to thank my brilliant and inspiring colleagues at SkyBridge. You work at the highest standards, and our customers and I are immensely grateful for that. A special shout-out to my partner and Ambassador to Coin, Brett Messing, who encouraged me to explore this exciting new world when others thought we were nuts. Your bravery knows no bounds.

There would be no Solana without the brilliant and visionary founders who had the courage to defy conventional wisdom and radically transform the crypto universe. Thank you, Anatoly Yakovenko and Raj Gokal, for your exceptional minds and determined grit. You've accomplished what so many can only dream of doing; you've changed the world. Thank you to the ever-thoughtful Kyle Samani of Multicoin. You've always been ahead of the pack, and your support and friendship are deeply valued.

I'd like to thank my many friends and supporters at CNBC, including KC Sullivan; my Squawk Box friends Andrew Ross Sorkin, Becky Quick, and Joe Kernen; as well as Anne Tironi and Jacqueline Corba. I'd especially like to thank my longtime friend and collaborator, Max Meyers. You understand my voice better than I do myself.

Most importantly, I want to thank the Scaramucci network, which is the source of everything that matters in my life. Thank you to my incredible wife, Deidre. You've made tomorrow's possibilities today's reality, and I can't imagine a moment without you. To my older children, AJ, Anthony, and Amelia, you never cease to amaze me. I've made countless mistakes in my life, but the manner in which you have all lived your lives ensures that I will always be a success. To my youngest sons, James and Nick, you amaze me every day with your love and brilliance. I look at you both and know the world will be a better place. Finally, to my mom, Marie, and late father, Alexander. With each passing day, it becomes clearer to me that I might have been the luckiest kid in all of Long Island—actually, the world. And what more could I say than that?

About the Author

Anthony Scaramucci is the founder and managing partner of SkyBridge Capital, a global alternative investment firm focusing on hedge funds, digital assets, and private equity. He founded SALT in 2009, a global thought leadership forum hosting events in New York, Singapore, and Abu Dhabi. Scaramucci began his career at Goldman Sachs and later founded Oscar Capital Management, which he eventually sold to Neuberger Berman in 2001. He all too briefly served as White House Communications Director in 2017. Scaramucci hosts the popular podcast *Open Book with Anthony Scaramucci*, featuring discussions with notable figures. He also co-hosts *The Rest Is Politics: US*. His recent books include *Hopping Over the Rabbit Hole*, *The Little Book of Bitcoin*, and *From Wall Street to the White House and Back*. In 2025, he was named to Crain's New York Notable Leaders in Finance for the second year. A Tufts and Harvard Law graduate, he lives in Manhasset, Long Island, with his wife, Deidre, and their children.

Index